# The nMRCGP Handbook

FREE

D1347681

# The nMRCGP Handbook

By

## Dr Bob Mortimer

QUAY
BOOKS

A division of MA Healthcare Ltd

Quay Books Division, MA Healthcare Ltd, St Jude's Church, Dulwich Road, London SE24 0PB

British Library Cataloguing-in-Publication Data
A catalogue record is available for this book

ISBN-10: 1-85642-359-X
ISBN-13: 978-1-85642-359-5

Printed in the UK by Ashford Colour Press, Gosport, Hants, PO13 0FW

# Contents

# About the author

Dr Bob Mortimer qualified from the Welsh National School of Medicine, Cardiff, in 1983. He passed the MRCGP in 1992, and became a Fellow of the Royal College of General Practitioners in 2005. He has been a GP trainer since 1995. In 1994 he set up the Swansea MRCGP Course and became an examiner in 1996, obtaining the Diploma in Medical Education (Cardiff) in 1998. Dr Mortimer was Associate Director for the Welsh Deanery until 2005.

Dr Mortimer is a full time GP and is an assessor for the Clinical Skills Assessment (CSA), and in addition to being a trainer for assessors he is also one of the senior marshals involved in the actual running of the CSA. He also runs the Swansea MRCGP Course.

*Acknowledgements*

*I would like to thank the Panel of Examiners for the MRCGP Examination, who have been the most inspiring group of people I have ever had the privilege to work with.*

# Foreword

I never enjoyed taking exams. Who does? But several decades ago, when I was coming to the end of my vocational training as a fledgling GP, I took the Membership of the Royal College of General Practitioners (MRCGP) Examination. I have never been a good judge of how I was doing during exams, and my pessimism was often justified. On this occasion I thought I was floundering. None of the questions had seemed straightforward, and my doubts and insecurity were increasing by the minute. And so, when the examiner asked me how I would deal with a patient who had been bitten by a dog shortly before boarding a plane in India the previous day, I just shrugged. *'I'm sorry'*, I said despairingly, *'I just don't know anything at all about rabies. I'd look it up'*.

But instead of groaning, both examiners grinned. One said: *'I've been asking this question for five days. You're the first one to give me the right answer'*.

And he was not joking. For a UK family doctor to treat possible rabies from memory would indeed be unsafe and unwise. Ultimately my result was better than I had ever dreamt of, and I decided this was a 'real-world' organisation that I could do business with. All too many examinations in the past seemed to have been built on theory alone. The Royal College of General Practitioners (RCGP) seemed to me to focus on the uncertain and unpredictable world that real GPs face with real patients, and over many years working with the RCGP, including 15 years as an examiner, my view has not changed.

That was then. This is now. The arrival of the Postgraduate Medical Education Training Board has led to the introduction of new curricula across every medical specialty, providing common standards, clarity and transparency to training, as well as promoting the continuous development of doctors' skills in order to meet patient need. General Practice, at long last, has now been recognised as a medical specialty equivalent to every other, and new assessment methodologies have been developed to match.

But change is always rather confusing, and it certainly feels threatening for learners as well as their trainers. At this time of great change in the MRCGP Examination, this book offers real insight and real support. Quite rightly, it stresses that the best way of passing the exam is by becoming a good GP. Exam technique, and understanding how exams work is important, but nothing counts for as much as being a caring, learning, and listening GP.

The nMRCGP is now a licensing exam. Every new GP in the UK will have to pass it. This is exactly how it should be — after all, being a GP is one of the most complex and skilled jobs in medicine, and it has always seemed insulting that lower mandatory standards were acceptable in our specialty. But now they are not. You have to pass, and the nation's patients deserve nothing less.

Reading this beautifully written, informative and supportive book will demystify many of the changes in the nMRCGP exam, and allows the reader to focus on what really matters — the patients and the care we can offer. High quality General Practice is of vital importance to patients everywhere. After all, good GPs really do make a difference.

*Professor David Haslam CBE, FRCP, FFPH, PRCGP*
*President of the Royal College of General Practitioners*

# Chapter 1

# Why do we need exams?

The aim of this book is to help you prepare for and pass the new membership exam for the Royal College of General Practitioners (*n*MRCGP). This introduction will explain why the exam is there and how it came about — the key to passing any examination is to get to know as much about it as you can. The book will describe the elements of the exam in some detail, with information on what each part is designed to assess and the methods with which it assesses you. There will be lots of practical advice on how to best prepare for the exam and how to ensure your best performance on the day.

There are no easy shortcuts to passing the *n*MRCGP, it is a highly rigorous assessment of your knowledge, clinical and communication skills and your ability to solve problems in general practice. Making sure you understand the exam will however mean that you can make efficient use of your time preparing for it. Much of your learning for the exam can be within your day-to-day experiences in your work, and the book will wherever possible advise you how to maximise the benefit you gain from these experiences and minimise the amount of the more traditional, and often less interesting, methods of preparing for an exam such as reading textbooks and journals. You will of course need to do some reading for the exam, but this book will help you to target the right material and use it efficiently.

## 1.1 Reasons for exams generally

By the time you get to sit the nMRCGP you will be quite an exam expert. You will have taken GCSEs at age 16 (or their equivalent where you were educated), A-levels or equivalent at age 18, followed by the various hurdles set in your way throughout medical school. Generally speaking the degree of difficulty rises as you progress through your career. There are several reasons for exams existing:

- To check that you have learned what you were supposed to in your course work
- To ensure suitability or ability to pursue a particular course of study
- To discriminate between applicants for a job or a place in a school or college
- To ensure you are up to scratch to do a particular job
- As a mark of status, or to demonstrate a level of excellence

Exams can test various things:

- Recalling of facts you are supposed to have learned
- Testing your ability to reason
- Solving problems
- Assessing your practical skills
- Checking some of your values and attitudes.

There are many different types of exams, and each type of exam will be more or less effective at assessing each of these attributes.

When you sit an exam it is important to have a clear idea of why you are taking it and what it is there to test. For the 'old' MRCGP exam points three and five in the list above were the most pertinent. In the case of the *n*MRCGP the fourth point becomes the most important as this is now a *licensing* examination, meaning that you will need to have passed the exam to practise as a GP in the UK.

## 1.2 The history of the MRCGP examination

The MRCGP has always been the examination to gain *membership* of the Royal College of General Practitioners (RCGP). Until 1968 a GP could join the College by simply paying a fee. Then along came the Membership exam and this became the only route to College membership. You did not *need* to become a member of the RCGP, and historically only just over half of trainee GPs took the exam and became members.

Those who took it did so for various reasons — some because they felt it was important to be a member of the College, but these were probably in the minority. Some took the exam as a personal challenge, and as an affirmation that they had attained a certain level of achievement following their vocational training. Some did it out of peer pressure, or because their course organiser or trainer expected them to do it. Probably the largest group were those who did it was because they thought it might improve their chances in job applications.

Initially the MRCGP comprised a multiple choice question paper (MCQ), a modified essay question paper (MEQ), a practice topic question paper (PTQ) and two oral examinations. Over the years these were gradually refined, often as a result of analysis and advice from the College's psychometric advisers — the MCQ stopped using negative marking as this discriminated against more timid candidates who were afraid to guess, and the true/false question format developed into extended matching questions and other question formats as this increased its ability to accurately discriminate between strong and weak candidates.

# 1.3 About the nMRCGP examination

Until 2007 doctors GP registrars in the UK had to satisfy the requirements of the Joint Committee on Postgraduate Training for General Practice (JCPTGP) by passing Summative Assessment. Some of the elements of Summative Assessment could be exempted by passing the appropriate modules of the MRCGP examination. The Government replaced the JCPTGP with a new body called the Postgraduate Medical Education and Training Board (PMETB, generally pronounced *pee-met-bee*). While the JCPTGP oversaw only training for general practice, the PMETB has responsibility for all the medical specialties.

The JCPTGP was called the Joint Committee as it was made up of representatives from both the Royal College of GPs and the General Practitioners Committee of the BMA (i.e. from the profession's academic body as well as from its 'trade union'). The vast majority of its members were GPs.

The PMETB is entirely different, with its members appointed by government and with 17 medical members (four of whom have a background in general practice) and eight lay members. It was decided that there was to be a new licensing examination for each medical specialty, and that this would be approved and overseen by the PMETB (DEpartment of Health [DH], 2001).

The RCGP followed the political developments closely and from an early stage started planning the new assessment. It was clear that any new assessment would need to be specifically designed to assess GP registrars at the end of training, and that simply presenting the existing exam would not be acceptable. The College has developed its curriculum for General Practice and this formed the basis for the new assessment which was designed to ensure that it tested all areas within the curriculum. For each area of the curriculum it was considered what form of test would be most fit for purpose. The RCGP curriculum will be covered in the next chapter.

The key challenges to the new examination were developing an assessment that was rigorous and robust enough to stand up to legal challenge; that had more emphasis than previous assessments on doctors' practical skills in consulting with and examining patients, and that assessed their progress through their training in a more structured and rigorous way. It also had to be able to assess the 3,000 or so doctors completing GP training each year.

There was a lot of discussion about the actual standard that was to be set — the MRCGP had previously had an overall pass rate of just over 70% while only a handful of doctors failed Summative Assessment each year. On the one hand it was felt that a pass rate of 98-99% was probably inappropriately high, while it was accepted that the implications of preventing almost 30% of registrars from entering general practice immediately after training were significant.

It was important from the outset that the new assessment must be ***criterion referenced***, meaning that it made an objective assessment of a doctor without comparison to everyone else taking the assessment. This makes standard setting even more important since it means that theoretically the assessment could fail everyone who took it.

The development of the new assessment has been led by various working groups comprised of members from both the College and the Deaneries across the UK, as well as having extensive input from lay representatives. The final product has three components:

- An applied knowledge test (AKT), which is a multiple choice type test
- The clinical skills assessment (CSA), which is a series of consultations with simulated patients.
- The workplace based assessment (WPBA); which is a structured assessment of the registrar's work in their training practice

The responsibility for the AKT and the CSA is largely held by the RCGP, with the Deaneries largely responsible for the WPBA.

A registrar will not 'qualify' as a GP until they have satisfactorily completed all three components (AKT, CSA, and WPBA). The WPBA is continuous throughout the all three yeras of training (see Chapter 4). AKT can be taken at any time during training but will usually be during the last year of training, and the CSA will need to be taken during the last year in general practice training.

## 1.4 The applied knowledge test

From the outset the AKT has been closely based on the 'old' MRCGP multiple choice questions paper, and is produced by the same group of assessors. There is little dispute that the multiple choice question format is the best suited to reliably test factual knowledge, and there were ample statistics to demonstrate that the nMRCGP MCQ could do this reliably. Reliability in this context means that a candidate's mark could be regarded as a true reflection of his or her ability, and that candidates of similar ability could be expected to achieve similar scores.

## 1.5 The clinical skills assessment

The CSA was devised to assess the practical skills that GPs needs, such as clinical examinations and communication.

Some envisaged this component as a form of OSCE in which candidates would visit stations at which they would be expected to demonstrate a specific skill, as commonly used in undergraduate medical exams. This, however, was felt to be too simplistic — it was felt that it was important to test integrative skills, meaning the ability to combine communication skills with clinical skills to gather information then to use medical knowledge and decision making skills to formulate a management plan. From an early stage it was considered that the best way to do this was using simulated patients. The MRCGP already had a simulated surgery module based on a series of consultations with simulated patients, but this was not felt to be a suitable model for the CSA and a working group set about planning the new assessment from scratch.

What they have finally come up with does look remarkably similar to the simulated surgery module — which is not exactly surprising given that both assessments were designed for the same purpose.

## 1.6 The workplace based assessment

To get a more holistic assessment of a registrar's competence it was felt that some form of in-training assessment was necessary. This has been present previously with the record of in-training assessment (RITAs) during hospital training and the trainer's report in general practice. Although the trainer's report was quite comprehensive and well structured, the WPBA is more rigorous with elements of external assessment and incorporates an objective assessment of consulting skills.

The GP trainer will collect evidence relating to the registrar's performance throughout their training. Much of this will be recorded by the trainer directly observing and recording the registrar's performance and progress, but there are several specific tools used to record and evaluate this:

■ Case-based discussion (CBD), which is a semi-structured interview based on cases
■ The consultation observation tool (COT), which is an objective assessment of consulting skills using a video of consultations
■ Multi-source feedback (MSF) via questionnaires from colleagues
■ Patient satisfaction questionnaires (PSQ)

The progress throughout the WBPA will be recorded in an electronic log, the ePortfolio, which is an electronic learning log used both as an educational tool and to record successful completion of the main elements (See chapter 4 for more information on the ePortfolio).

**References**

DH (2001) *Postgraduate Medical Education and Training*. Department of Health, London

# Chapter 2

# The RCGP curriculum

## 2.1 What is the curriculum?

Essentially, the RCGP curriculum sets out what you need to learn throughout GP training. It aims to cover all the areas described in *Good Medical Practice* (General Medical Council [GMC], 2006). The curriculum is divided up into six separate domains of competence, and within each of these domains the authors have defined a series of learning outcomes. The six domains are as follows:

- Primary care management
- Person-centred care
- Specific problem-solving skills
- A comprehensive approach
- Community orientation
- A holistic approach

You can see that although these domains include the factual knowledge required to be a GP, many of them refer more to skills and attitudes.

This chapter may seem a bit unnecessary, but it is important as it defines everything you need to know to pass the exam, and throughout the sections of the book describing the various parts of the exam I will refer back to the domains and some of the learning outcomes.

The following sections will describe the domains but do not give comprehensive details or listings of all the learning outcomes related to each as these can be downloaded easily from the RCGP website (See Resources section at the end of this chapter).

As you read them you may think that there is significant overlap between some of the domains, and you would be right as there certainly is overlap. Do not be put off by this and do not be put off by the complexity of the curriculum — it is recommended that you read through the College's *Curriculum Guide for Learners and Teachers,* but do not try to memorise it. The whole curriculum is long and detailed and is only really useful to you as reference material rather than as primary reading material. It defines the scope of what the examination sets out to assess you on but is not necessarily terribly useful to you as revision material.

### 2.1.1 Primary care management

This domain is about the way in which GPs have to be able to deal with anything presented to them; there is generally no filtering before a patient sees a GP and the problem can be from any area within medicine.

The way in which a GP interfaces with the health service is also important, making effective use of services provided by other professionals both within the practice and in secondary care. A GP has to balance doing his best for an individual patient whilst managing resources effectively.

This means the GP needs to have the medical knowledge to deal with acute and chronic conditions, prevent them, palliative care and medical emergencies. To effectively manage these conditions will require communication, clinical examination and therapeutic skills as well as the ability to prioritise. A GP also has to understand how primary care and the wider NHS is organised and needs to be able to work in a team and demonstrate leadership. Use of information technology and an understanding of audit are also important.

This domain describes the concept of patient advocacy, which means communicating with each person as an equal and representing his/her interests with respect to the NHS and other organisation (for example employers, and the Benefits Agency). This must of course be tempered with equality and distributive justice.

The learning outcomes for this domain are knowledge and skill based. You should have sufficient knowledge of the range of illnesses encountered in primary care, as well as understanding of the structure and organisation of the NHS. You should also have organisational, clinical and communication skills, as well as effective teamwork both within the practice and in the interface with secondary care.

---

**Learning points: primary care management**

- Medical knowledge
- IT and audit
- Communication
- Ability to prioritise
- Organisational knowledge
- Teamworking

---

### 2.1.2 Person-centred care

The curriculum describes the following three principles:

■ Committing to the person rather than to a particular body of knowledge

■ Seeking to understand the context of the illness
■ Attaching importance to the subjective aspects of medicine

This domain is about treating the person rather than the illness, making sure that you fully appreciate the patient's perspective on the problem and incorporates his/her patient's preferences and expectations into any management plan. It does not of course mean simply doing what the patient wants since this may not actually be in the patient's best interests or there may be issues relating to limited resources, including your time. It does however mean that you should be able to deal with these issues in a way that maintains a good relationship with the patient.

Continuity of care is also key to this domain, maintaining a long-term relationship with a patient, acting in partnership and making shared decisions rather than being paternalistic and making decisions on the patient's behalf.

While knowledge does feature in the learning outcomes for this domain, the emphasis is more on attitude and the communication skills required to fully explore the patient's agenda and integrate the patient's ideas, concerns and expectations into a management plan.

It can be helpful to consider consultation models in this domain. The most obviously applicable is that commonly known as *Pendleton*, described in the book *The Consultation – An Approach to Teaching and Learning* and which also discusses the importance of establishing the patient's ideas, concerns and expectations (Pendleton et al, 1984). This has had a profound influence on the development of assessment of communication skills in the MRCGP exam.

In his book *The Inner Consultation,* Neighbour (2004) describes connecting, that is, establishing a relationship and rapport with the patient where the doctor summarises his understanding of the patient's problem back to him to check that he has understood the patient correctly. He finally describes handing over, which includes negotiating a mutually acceptable management plan.

---

**Learning points: person-centred care**

- Attitude and communication
- Exploring the patient's agenda
- Care management and planning
- Consultation models

---

### 2.1.3 Specific problem-solving skills

When we learn to consult patients as medical students and junior doctors, we use a systematic approach using a series of questions to cover the whole of a patient's past medical history and all of their clinical systems. This then leads into what is generally referred to as a specialist approach where more detailed examinations and investigations are used to narrow down the problem and reduce uncertainty by systematically excluding conditions.

However this approach does not work in general practice, and not only because we do not have the time in a general practice consultation to use it. In general practice we need to adopt a more problem-based approach where we attempt to focus down very quickly on the patient's problem, using our knowledge of the prevalence of conditions to direct and focus our history taking and examination. We make decisions based on probability and must accept a degree of uncertainty, often using time to clarify the problem. We analyse and attempt to reduce risks whilst recognising that we cannot completely exclude them, and we must always recognise the need to act urgently where required. This is known as a generalist approach.

Apart from saving time, the advantages of a generalist approach include protecting patients from unnecessary and sometimes unpleasant investigations, as well as the consequent saving of resources. There is also the issue of anxiety — doing more investigations has clearly been shown to make patients more worried about the possibility of serious illnesses.

The learning outcomes for this domain include knowledge of the incidence and prevalence of diseases and the application of this to an individual patient's social and family context. Knowledge of investigations and treatments available and of their usefulness, as well as their cost, is also important. The skills required are those needed to gather the appropriate information by taking a history and examining the patient, being able to use the information gained, applying clinical reasoning and making sensible decisions. They also include the skills required to recognise when it is OK to watch and wait, and when it is important to act promptly.

---

**Learning points: specific problem-solving skills**

- Knowledge of incidence and prevalence of conditions
- Knowledge of investigations and costs
- History-taking and data gathering
- Applying clinical reasoning
- Decision-making

---

### 2.1.4 A comprehensive approach

Patients rarely present with single isolated problems, and this domain is about managing multiple problems, managing problems within the patient's psychosocial context and integrating preventive medicine and health promotion into the consultation. As a GP you must also provide ongoing care for chronic conditions and in the rehabilitation phase of illnesses.

Learning outcomes for this domain include knowledge of the concept of health and wellbeing, health promotion and of the complexity of problems in general practice.

The skills of managing multiple morbidities and being able to promote health both within the individual consultation and more broadly are also important.

---

**Learning points: a comprehensive approach**

- Knowledge of health and wellbeing
- Health promotion

---

### 2.1.5 Community orientation

GPs work within a defined community and it is important to understand the socioeconomic and health features of that community. This domain describes the need to reconcile the needs of the individual patient with those of the community, matched up with the resources available.

The learning outcomes associated with this domain are largely knowledge based — an understanding of the socioeconomic features of the local community and understanding the way they influence health. These factors include poverty, ethnicity, rurality and the area's industrial/commercial history. You should also know the local variations within the healthcare and social services in the area, as well as understanding the roles of other professionals working locally.

---

**Learning points: community orientation**

- Understanding of socioeconomic features
- Understanding and knowledge of local community
- Knowledge of local variations in healthcare other social services
- Understanding of the role of other local healthcare professionals

---

### 2.1.6 A holistic approach

The concept of holism is an important one to general practice, particularly in the UK where continuing care in long-term relationships with patients is a key feature. Holism means treating the whole patient, considering other issues rather than the purely medical; for instance the person's values which might be based on their culture, ethnicity, religion and the way their family structure influences them. The integration of the physical, psychological and social components of health problems has been well demonstrated to be related to longer consultations and to better continuity of care (Freeman et al, 2002). It is perhaps difficult to reconcile this with modern general practice where continuity is decreasing and quality of care tends to be measured by how quickly a patient can get an appointment than the length of the consultation.

Holism also implies a broader view of interventions, combining psychological, physical and sometimes complementary therapies with the traditional pharmacological ones.

Learning outcomes for this domain include knowledge of holism and how a person's social and psychological circumstances impinge on health as well as knowledge of the patient's cultural background and beliefs.

Skill is required to integrate this knowledge into the care of the patient, and attitude aspects such as tolerance and understanding of a patient's beliefs and values are important.

---

**Learning points: a holistic approach**

- Knowledge of psychological, physical and complementary therapies
- Understanding of holism
- Tolerance of patient's beliefs and values

---

### References

Freeman G, Horder J, Howle J, et al (2002) Evolving general practice consultation in Britain: issues of length and context. *BMJ* 324: 880–82

GMC (2006) *Good Medical Practice*. General Medical Council, London

Neighbour R, et al (2004) *The Inner Consultation: How to Develop an Effective and Intuitive Consulting Style*. Radcliffe Publishing, London

Pendleton D, et al (1984) *The Consultation — An Approach to Teaching and Learning*. Oxford University Press, Oxford

### Resources

**General Medical Council**: www.gmc-uk.org

**Royal College of General Practitioners**: www.rcgp.org

# Chapter 3

# The Applied Knowledge Test

As is obvious from its name, the AKT is a test of knowledge. What the word 'applied' adds is the explicit statement that it is not simply a test of the simpler 'building blocks' of knowledge you might have, but that the exam tests how you might apply your knowledge to general practice. The knowledge you need is very specific to general practice, rather than just theoretical medical knowledge.

For example, rather than simply asking about heart failure, a question might ask about a specific patient, giving a clinical scenario with information about age, sex, specific investigation results and treatment the patient is already on.

The knowledge tested is that required by a working GP in the UK, so it encompasses all the basic knowledge gained throughout medical training but very definitely seeks to test up-to-date evidence-based medicine, therapeutics and current nationally accepted guidelines.

Clearly in a single examination it is impossible to test that a candidate knows everything he/she might need to know as a GP. So the examiners use sampling — dividing the curriculum up into logical areas and asking questions from each area.

To make sure that the questions asked adequately represent the breadth of the curriculum requires an adequate sample of questions from each curriculum area, and the more questions the examiners ask the more confident they can be that they have adequately covered the curriculum. There is a limit of course to how many questions they can reasonably ask in a single examination session, so the compromise is reached with a three hour 'paper' and about 200 questions.

## 3.1 Exam format and logistics

The MRCGP MCQ was always computer marked, but for the AKT the College is taking this a step further by making the entire test computer-based.

Each candidate will sit the test at a computer station, selecting the correct answers with mouse-clicks instead of the traditional method of shading lozenges in with a pencil on a piece of paper. This has several implications for both the College and you as the candidate. For the candidate it removes the potential for errors shading lozenges (they had to be shaded in accurately and there was a risk of shading a lozenge in the wrong row). For the College the most obvious benefit is that the answers can be directly entered into a database thereby removing the risk of misreading the answer sheet.

There are, however, deeper implications than this. Logistically there is a problem being able to provide sufficient computer stations for the expected 3,000 plus candidates per year. This is solved by using Pearson Vue, best known to most as the company who run the centres at which the UK driving theory test is held. The AKT will be held at Pearson Vue's 147 test centres across the UK on three days per year. Places will be allocated on a first come first served basis, so an early application is recommended if you want to sit it at the centre of your choice.

Despite the shift in delivery method, the examination will be essentially the same as the MRCGP MCQ in terms of length of the exam, number of questions, question format and the areas covered. The College has significantly increased its bank of questions, allowing different questions to be used each time to reduce the impact of candidates memorising questions and passing them on to colleagues. This, along with high levels of security, means that you are unlikely to encounter 'genuine' AKT questions either in books, on courses or on websites.

### 3.1.1 When to sit the AKT

It is currently envisaged that in order to pass the nMRCGP, each component must be successfully completed within three years of passing the first component but at the time of writing the College has not taken a firm decision on this. Similarly a firm decision on the number of attempts that can be made has not yet been made. However this information will be easily available on the College's website.

It is important to choose the best time to sit the exam; sit it too soon and you run an increased risk of failure as you may not have gained the requisite knowledge. Clearly a candidate is likely to perform best at the end of training, but a failure then may leave no time to re-sit and thus may delay qualification as a GP.

The College recommends that candidates sit the AKT in the third year of training, ST3, but which sitting to attempt must be an individual decision for each registrar based on confidence in his/her own level of preparation and with some input from the trainer. Although much (but not all) of the clinical medicine will have been learned before the year in general practice, it is likely that most of the critical appraisal and administration questions will require knowledge gained in general practice. Bear in mind that even material learned while in secondary care may well need to be reconsidered in a general practice context.

The College plans to make results available shortly after each sitting of the AKT, but it has not yet released the exact details.

## 3.2 Question formats

The AKT uses several different question formats. The traditional format for medical multiple choice questions was the true/false type where there was typically a description of a question area followed by five different statements each of which were either true or false. This naturally meant that there was a roughly 50% chance of guessing any question correctly even with no medical knowledge.

To counter this negative marking was introduced, meaning that a correct answer scored plus one mark, a wrong answer scored a minus one mark, with no mark if the question was left unanswered. Negative marking was dropped after it was made clear that it discriminated against less confident candidates as they would leave blank any questions they were unsure of, whereas the more confident candidates would guess them. In any examination the goal is to accurately discriminate between the good candidates and the weaker ones, and reducing the odds of correctly guessing an answer to below 50% increases this discrimination. The College abandoned the multiple true/false format in the early 90s and no questions in this format will appear in the AKT.

The following is the list of questions formats used, although it is entirely possible that new formats could appear at any time:

- Extended matching questions
- Single best answer
- Multiple best answers
- Picture format
- Table/algorithm completion
- Data interpretation
- Seminal trials

During the exam a simple example will be given for each format purely to demonstrate the format, and more are available on the College's website.

### 3.2.1 Extended matching questions

In this question format a range of options are provided as answers, and each separate question is a short scenario. You must choose the correct answer from the range of options for each scenario. Each answer carries one mark.

It will be specified that **only one** option is correct. Although you may consider more than one option to be plausible, one will be the single most appropriate answer. This will generally be based on an authoritative source such as the *British National Formulary* (BNF), a nationally recognised guideline or a piece of important published research.

You can see from the example box that using this format means random guesses would be expected to yield a mark of 12.5%.

### 3.2.2 Single best answer

The odds are a little better here at 1 in 7, but the question is made more difficult

## Example: Extended matching questions

**Theme: Management of hypertension**

*Option list:*

- Lifestyle advice
- Bendroflumethiazide
- Atenolol
- Lisinopril
- Irbesartan
- Methyldopa
- Nifedipine
- Doxazosin

**Instruction:**

For each patient with hypertension select the single most appropriate treatment. Each answer may be used once, more than once, or not at all.

*Items:*

- A 79 year old non-diabetic patient with no significant past medical history and repeated blood pressure readings averaging 155/85
- A 79 year old diabetic patient with repeated blood pressure readingsaveraging 155/85
- A 57 year old Afro-Caribbean man with repeated blood pressure readings averaging 155/85 who is already taking indapamide 2.5mg daily

## Example: Single best answer

According to current evidence, which treatment provides the greatest benefit in premenstrual syndrome? Select one answer only

- Fluoxetine
- Mefenamic acid
- Norethisterone
- The combined oral contraceptive pill
- Evening primrose oil
- Depo-provera
- Vitamin B6

by more than one option appearing plausible. More than one of these treatments has been claimed or shown to be effective in premenstrual syndrome, but recent evidence suggests one to be superior to the others. See example box.

### 3.2.3 Multiple best answers

This is similar to the single best answer format but where you are asked to specify a given number of options.

In the example box given, each answer carries one mark, the order in which you choose them does not matter. Although you might think the odds reduce from 1 in 10 to 1 in 9 once you have made your first choice that is only true if you have got the first one right.

---

**Example: Multiple best answer**

According to the NICE guidelines for management of feverish illness in children which THREE of the following features are NOT classified within the RED category:

*Option List:*

- Non-blanching rash
- Dry mucous membrane
- Appears ill to a healthcare professional
- Oxygen saturation ≤95% in air
- Weak, high pitched or continuous cry
- Grunting
- Respiratory rate >40 breaths/minute age > 12 months
- Bile-stained vomiting
- Focal neurological signs
- Age 0-3 months, temperature >=38°C

---

### 3.2.4 Table/algorithm completion

In this more graphical question format you are provided with a table or an algorithm (a chart usually depicting a clinical care pathway) where some of the text has been removed. You need to select the appropriate option for each space from a list. See example box on the next page.

Again in this case the odds of guessing are low, at 1 in 8 for each item, although some are easily excluded. We will discuss strategies for answering questions in a later section.

## Example: Table/algorithm completion

**The UK Resusciattion Council Automated external defibrillator resuscitation (AED) algorithm**

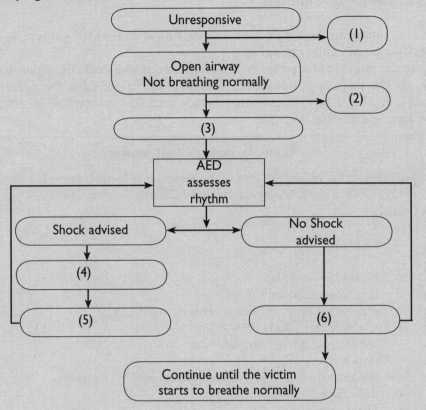

For each of the numbered gaps select **ONE** option from the list below. Each option may be used once, more than once, or not at all. Select **ONE** option only.

a. Check for pulse
b. CPR 30:2 until AED is attached
c. Immediately resume CPR 30:2 for 2 minutes
d. Administer oral aspirin
e. Send or go for AED. Call 999
f. 1 shock 150-360J biphasic or 360J monophasic
g. Call for help
h. Insert oral airway

## Example: Data interpretation

**The following data is from a trial of a new screening test for carcinoma of the prostate. The numbers represent the number of patients in the trial for each category**

|  | Disease | No Disease | Total |
|---|---|---|---|
| Positive test | 4 | 1 | 5 |
| Negative test | 2 | 93 | 95 |
| Total | 6 | 94 | 100 |

Option list: The numbers below reflect the numbers from the table as fractions

a. 4/5
b. 1/5
c. 2/95
d. 93/95
e. 2/93
f. 6/100
g. 6/94
h. 93/100

i. 94/100
j. 95/100
k. 5/95
l. 5/100
m. 4/6
n. 2/6
o. 1/94
p. 93/94
q. none of these

For each of the following items select the most appropriate answer from the options list above.

Items:

1. The sensitivity of the test
2. The specificity of the test
3. The positive predictive value of the test
4. The negative predictive value of the test
5. The prevalence of the disease among the sample of the trial

### 3.2.5 Data interpretation

In this format the examiners can assess your ability to understand various presentations of statistical data. This may be in the form of a series of numbers, data table, or any of the graphical presentations of data such as graphs, bar charts, Forest plots, and so on. It is clear here that you must have a good understanding of the statistical terms referred to — if you do the questions are quite easy. We will discuss the terms and graphical presentation methods you need to know about in a later section. Consider the example in page 19. This format of question can be quite difficult to grasp, especially in the stress of an exam, so perhaps it will be helpful to go through this example in a little more detail. The table shows data from an imaginary trial of a screening test for carcinoma of the prostate. Let's first of all just clarify what the rows and column in the table mean. The top row shows the number of patients who had a positive test with the total on the far right (5). The row below shows those who had a negative test again with the total on the far right (95), thus the total number in this trial was 100, which is shown in the bottom right cell. The numbers are subdivided into two columns depending on whether the patients actually did have the disease or not, with totals on the bottom row.

The right hand column tells you that of these 100 patients 5 had a positive test while the remaining 95 were negative. The bottom row tells you that of the 100 patients 6 were known to have the disease while the remaining 94 did not. The left column tells you that of these 6 patients with the disease, 4 had a positive test while the other two tested negative. The middle column tells you that 1 patient who did not have the disease had a positive test, while the remaining 93 disease-free patients tested negative.

Moving on to the question items, the first one, the sensitivity of the test, refers to the proportion of true positives that are correctly identified by the test. In this example we can see that there were 6 true positives of whom 4 were correctly identified. Therefore the answer is 4/6 which is option '*m*'.

Item two asks for the specificity of the test which refers to the proportion of true negatives that are correctly identified by the test. Here we have 94 true negatives of whom 93 correctly had a negative test so the answer is 93/94 which is option '*p*'.

Item three asks for the positive predictive value. This is the reliability with which a positive test correctly identifies a patient with the disease. In this example there were 5 positive tests of whom 4 actually had the disease, so the positive predictive value is 4/5. option '*a*'.

The negative predictive value in item four refers to the reliability with which a negative test identifies a patient who does not have the disease. Here there were 95 patients who tested negative of whom 93 were actually disease free giving a negative predictive value of 93/95.

Item five asks for the prevalence of the disease in the study population. This is simply the number who did have the disease as a proportion of the total, in this case 6 out of 100, option '*f*'.

### 3.2.6 Seminal trials

This format allows the examiners to test knowledge previously tested in written papers. It allows them to test knowledge of very specific clinical trials, which can include very recent data.

For this sort of question you are likely to be asked about any relevant aspects of the methodology and about the results. Do not worry too much about remembering dates, authors, the journal articles were published, etc.

---

**Example: Seminal trial**

**Regarding the Scandinavian Simvastatin Survival Study (Lancet 1994; 344: 1383-89)**

Which **THREE** of the following statements is correct:

a. This study is an example of primary prevention
b. The follow-up period was over 5 years
c. There was no difference in non-cardiovascular deaths
d. The trial results were published as absolute risk reductions
e. There was a significant reduction in all-cause mortality in women
f. The absolute risk reductions for those aged over 65 years were roughly double that for the aged under 65 years
g. This was a cohort study
h. The study was a randomised controlled trial
i. The NNT for mortality was 12

---

## 3.3 Question areas

About 80% of the questions in the AKT are on clinical medicine, 10% on critical appraisal and evidence-based medicine and the remaining 10% on health informatics and administration.

### 3.3.1 Clinical medicine

The problem with clinical medicine is that as GPs we see undifferentiated problems, and as patients can turn up with *any* problem, you might think you need to know *everything*. Clearly that is simply not feasible, so the trick in preparing for the exam is to be selective. Looking through the examiners' comments on the College website can be quite illuminating in considering how the examiners choose the topics for questions. The important thing to remember is that this is an exam about *general practice*, so it is important to know a lot about the things we see frequently, but it is reasonable to expect a lower level of knowledge for the rarer problems. This presents a bit of a dilemma though from a safety point of view — what about the patient who turns up with something rare but with potentially serious consequences? The answer is of course that we need to know enough about the less common but serious problems to be able to spot them when they do present; we must have good self-awareness about the areas in which we are weaker and we need to recognise an ill patient who needs urgent action.

Considering the various areas described in the curriculum can be helpful. They can be divided according to which clinical system they affect:

- Cardiovascular problems
- Digestive problems
- Drug and alcohol problems
- ENT and facial problems
- Eye problems
- Metabolic problems
- Neurological problems
- Respiratory problems
- Rheumatology and conditions of the musculoskeletal system (including trauma)
- Skin problems (dermatology)

The curriculum also discusses these areas in groupings according to age/sex, and a couple of broader clinical areas:

- Healthy people: promoting health and preventing disease
- Genetics in primary care
- Care of acutely ill people
- Care of children and young people
- Care of older adults
- Gender-specific health issues
- Women's health
- Men's health
- Sexual health
- Care of people with cancer and palliative care
- Care of people with mental health problems
- Care of people with learning disabilities

### 3.3.2 Critical appraisal and evidence-based medicine

Critical appraisal is the skill of being able to read a piece of material and appraise it from several points of view. Try asking yourself the following questions when appraising material: is it relevant to me as a GP?; Is the methodology appropriate to the aims of the work?; Is there any bias?; Are the findings significant and are the conclusions appropriate to the findings?

Relevance is important — this can be about how common or important the subject matter is to general practice or it can be about the context of the work, for example studies done in secondary care.

It is important to understand the various kind of methodology used in studies. The following is a list of the main methodologies:

- *Case report or series*

A report on a single case or a limited number of cases, generally where something unusual has happened.

An example of this would be a report of a patient suffering unexpected side effects from a drug.

- *Cohort study*

A longitudinal study where a specific group of subjects are followed up over a period of time to observe what happens to them.

An example of this would be following up a group of patients with a raised PSA to observe the incidence of prostatic carcinoma. There would usually be a control group (of patients with a normal PSA) for comparison. Note that this methodology is *prospective*.

- *Case control study*

This is where individuals with a condition are matched with controls who do not have the condition but who are similar in other ways (e.g. age, sex).

An example would be looking at patients with breast cancer and comparing them with similar controls to identify potential risk factors. Note that this methodology is *retrospective*. See below for further discussion of this. Note also that any factors identified are *associations* rather than necessarily being *causes*.

- *Prospective study*

This is a study in which all the study parameters are defined and study population identified before the intervention is applied or before they are divided into groups and observed longitudinally. This includes all randomised trials and some cohort studies.

- *Retrospective study*

The study parameters are defined, then the researchers look back at what has already happened to the study population. This includes most case control studies and retrospective cohort studies. While retrospective studies have the advantage that they can often be done quickly (since all the data is generally already available) the disadvantage is that there is potentially more risk of bias or confunding.

- *Uncontrolled trial*

Where a group of subjects are subjected to an intervention (such as a drug treatment) and followed up to observe the effect. A drawback with this methodology is that any observed improvements (or deteriorations) may have arisen anyway and may not necessarily be as a result of the intervention.

- *Randomised control trial*

This is the better method of investigating the effects of an intervention. The subjects are allocated at random to receive either the intervention or to be controls. The control group may receive no intervention, a placebo or a different form of intervention (for instance where a new drug is compared with the current usual therapy for a condition).

- *Systematic review*

This is a form of review where the researcher looks for all relevant research articles on a subject and analyses them to produce a summary.

- *Meta-analysis*

This is similar to a systematic review but the researcher actually combines the raw data gathered in the original research articles and combines it all to produce a single large dataset. This is useful when studies show very small effects or where results of different studies are conflicting, often as a result of studies being small and lacking power. The randomised controlled trial and the meta-analysis are considered the *gold standard* for evidence-based medicine.

### 3.3.3 Qualitative research

The methodologies described above are mostly quantitative, that is they produce numbers which can be analysed statistically. Some research subjects are not suitable to this approach however, for example where the researchers are investigating peoples' views on a subject, or investigating the effect an illness. Typically they involve questionnaires and interviews to generate their information.

There are several types of *bias* that can afflict clinical papers.

**Selection bias** is where the people being studied are in some way selected and not necessarily representative of the general population. Examples include studies on students, prisoners, or volunteers, or where certain groups (for example the elderly) are excluded form a study.

**Information bias** is caused by data gathering having a subjective element.

**Observer bias** is a form of information bias where measurements taken may not be consistent depending on who takes them. **Inter-observer bias** would be for example where different clinicians taking the same measurement on the same patient would obtain different values. **Intra-observer** bias is where the same clinician obtains different values, for example checking the same patient's blood pressure several times within a few minutes and recording different readings.

**Recall bias is** another source of information bias, where subjects are asked to recall what has happened. For example, asking patients how long they waited for their doctor to arrive when they called with chest pain.

**Confounding bias** is where factors other than the ones being studied may account for an observed effect. For example, the finding that beer drinkers are more likely to suffer from lung cancer than non-beer drinkers. The confounding factor here of course is that it is likely the beer drinkers are more likely to be smokers than the non-beer drinkers.

Statistics causes many registrars a headache but in reality you probably do not need to know as much as you think you might. One of the most common problems encountered is that most statistical textbooks, even the fairly basic ones provide more depth than is needed, which causes confusion. It is easy to read a chapter and think you have understood it only to find 10 minutes later that you cannot remember it. The solution here is to limit your learning to the basics.

Here is my list of the terms and concepts you should try to make sure you understand:

- Normal distribution and what the terms median and mode mean
- Probability, including *p* values and confidence intervals
- Correlation, including what a *chi-squared test* is for
- Sensitivity, specificity, positive and negative predictive values
- Relative and absolute risk reduction, including the ability to calculate numbers needed to treat (NNT) from some simple figures
- Odds ratios

Make sure you are aware of the common ways of presenting statistical data, such as graphs showing positive or negative correlation, and Forest plots. There is an excellent BMJ article which explains them fully (Lewis and Clarke, 2001). In the old style MRCGP knowledge of the points above were often asked in the critical reading questions within the written paper. Look through the past papers on the College website to see some example of statistic depth required for the exam.

This section has just been a short summary of research methodologies and critical appraisal, and a more detailed discussion is beyond the scope of this book. There are plenty of resources for learning about critical appraisal; see the resource section at the end of this chapter for examples.

The sources used for the evidence-based medicine questions will be discussed in a later section.

## 3.4 Health informatics and administration

Modern general practice is heavily dependent on information technology. This requires an understanding of computers, clinical coding, searching data and data management. The RCGP recommends that registrars should have reached the standard of the European Computer Driving Licence (ECDL) by the end of their GP training programme. Make sure you know about this (See the Resources section at the end of this chapter).

The term *information governance* describes the management of confidentiality in an electronic world. It is important that you have an awareness of the legislation covering this in the UK — you do not need to know the legalese in depth but you need to be aware of the implications for the GP in his daily work. Find out who the Caldicott Guardian is in your practice and speak to them about what their role entails. Make sure you understand the issues relating to use of patient records for reports to third parties such as insurance companies etc. and the Data Protection Act 1998.

You can do most of the revision on health informatics and administration you need for the *n*MRCGP from your computer. Make sure you understand how to make the most of it, consider how and why you use each internet-based tool.

Other questions in this section relate to aspects of general practice administration. The following lists some of the ones you need to know about:

- Sickness certification
- Fitness to drive guidelines
- Employment law
- Health and safety at work
- Control of substances hazardous to health (CoSHH) legislation
- The GMS contract and quality and outcomes (QOF) framework

These will not be detailed in this book as it is very easy to source the information you need from the internet.

## 3.5 How to prepare for the paper

The sure way to pass the AKT is to know everything there is to know in the curriculum areas.

However this is not possible, and the reason you are reading this book is to improve your chances of passing the exam with the minimal expenditure of time and effort.

There are two ways a book like this can help you — firstly by giving guidance on how to make the best use of your revision time and secondly by giving advice on examination technique. This section will deal with the former, while examination technique will be covered in the last section in this chapter.

### 3.5.1 Key topics

Adult education should be specific to the learner, identifying their needs and meeting them in ways that suit their learning style. However, no doubt at the start of your practice year your trainer will have identified some key basics that you would need to cover.

The same principle applies to the AKT; there are some topics that it is worth listing and revising systematically as they are very likely to come up in the exam. The list below is focused on those topics that are relatively easy to revise as they are fairly finite topics and they have very specific, definitive resources that you can access easily.

- Guidelines (e.g. NICE/SIGN)
- National Service Frameworks
- Fitness to drive guidance
- Drug interactions
- *BNF* guidance on prescribing
- *Drug and Therapeutics Bulletin*
- Key legislation
- Key *BMJ* articles

**Guidelines** — the National Institute for Clinical Effectiveness (NICE) and the Scottish Intercollegiate Guidelines Network (SIGN) are bodies which regularly publish nationally accepted guidelines. Although both organisations do publish paper copies of their work, they both have up-to-date, well maintained websites with easy access to all their guidance.

Have a good look at both sites and look through the guidelines published within the last couple of years. Some will have little or no relevance to general practice, so exercise judgement as to which ones you think it is worth spending some time on. As discussed earlier concentrate on both the topics that you commonly deal with as a GP and those that are less common but important to get right. It is worth writing a summary of each and keeping these together so you can read through your summary again. If you have friends locally who are also preparing for the exam you can pool efforts by allocating the various guidelines among yourselves and sharing the summaries you produce. Actually discussing them in a group session makes it more likely you will remember the information.

In addition there are a few key guidelines published by other bodies, particularly the medical Royal Colleges. These include the British Thoracic Society guidelines for asthma in adults and children and the British Hypertension Society guidelines (see resources section).

**National Service Frameworks** — these are again published by NICE and you should be familiar with those published so far. These currently include:

**Fitness to drive** — guidance is published by the Driver and Vehicle Licensing Agency (DVLA) and while there will probably be a paper copy in your practice, the most recent guidance can be downloaded from the DVLA website in PDF format. Again there is a bit too much here to learn it all but make sure you know the areas that are likely to crop up in your work as a GP. These include myocardial infarction and angina, epilepsy and other causes of loss of consciousness, TIA and stroke.

**Drug interactions** — these have always been a regular feature in the MRCGP MCQ and it seems likely they will remain so in the AKT. They have always been an important topic but current chronic disease management encourages polypharmacy like never before, thereby making interactions more important than ever. Again you cannot really just revise the whole BNF section on interactions so you must be selective. The general principal remains that you must focus on the common ones and on those that are potentially serious. Make sure you read up on interactions with warfarin, oral contraceptives and anticonvulsants particularly. A related area is that of drugs that are particularly likely to cause side-effects or which require specific monitoring such as the disease modifying anti-rheumatic drugs.

**The BNF** — in addition to looking up specific items it is well worth spending an hour or two reading through the sections containing guidance on prescribing at the front of the book. This includes guidance on prescription writing, emergency supply of medicines, controlled drugs, adverse reactions, prescribing for children, the elderly and in palliative care and emergency treatment of poisoning. Each section also has specific prescribing advice although this may be best read when you look up individual drugs.

**Drug and Therapeutics Bulletin** — this is now published by the BMJ Group, is independent of government and the NHS, and is highly respected as an authoritative source of prescribing information. It is published fortnightly and it is well worth looking through the last 12 to 18 months' issues to identify any topics you think look important. It is available online but you will need either a BMA subscription or an Athens username and password to access it. As a GP registrar you should be able to have access, so ask your trainer about it.

**Key legislation** — there are aspects of legislation that are important and worth summarising for revision — as mentioned already make sure you know about the Data Protection Act, Access to Medical Records Act, Health and Safety at Work, COSHH and advance directives.

**The British Medical Journal** — is a major source of information for the nMRCGP. Lots of questions are based on *BMJ* articles, particularly the educational ABC series and themed issues. The *BMJ* website organises these nicely for you.

### 3.5.2 Identifying educational needs

Identifying your educational needs is of great importance when the amount of potential material as so vast and your time is limited.

The first opportunity we will discuss is what is called *experiential learning* which is basically learning by experiences. The trouble is that you do not learn purely from experience, but the experience of seeing patients and working in a primary care team provides you with daily prompts of the things you do not know so well as you should. Make sure you switch autopilot off and think about everything you do. Hopefully as a registrar you have enough breathing space to be able to reflect between consultations. Keep a notebook with you and jot down any knowledge gaps you spot during the working day.

The term *PUNS and DENs* was coined in the early 90s by Richard Eve, a GP Tutor who described the process of identifying when you had encountered a knowledge gap (**P**atient's **U**nmet **N**eed) and by jotting it down and reflecting upon it later to convert it into a focused educational need (**D**octor's **E**ducational **N**eed) (Eve, 2003).

For every diagnosis think of the differential — are you confident of the aetiology of the illness, any diagnostic criteria and appropriate investigations? Are there any guidelines for referral or management?

Think about every prescription — doctors often prescribe a drug because it is what they are comfortable with, often because it was a consultant's 'favourite' drug during the early formative months in their medical career, however the drug might well be the correct choice but we should always be consciously aware of why we are prescribing it, what the benefits of the individual drug are and of the potential risks of prescribing it.

Another opportunity for identifying learning needs is in your general reading and keeping up-to-date with current journals. Doctors have a habit of sticking to what they know, but you need to learn the habit of identifying topics you think you do not know enough about.

Scan the *BMJ* weekly, again being selective to identify articles of relevance to you. Do not just read the editorials, research articles and the ABC series; the news pages often have reports on important work published elsewhere such as the *New England Journal of Medicine* and the *Lancet*. Any obvious important papers are likely to be discussed in the editorial and are likely to be discussed in the weekly magazines such as *GP*, *Pulse* and *Doctor*. The letters section has always been useful to students for critical appraisal, and the online journal allows for the fairly interactive *rapid responses* which make the debate much more real-time.

### 3.5.3 Meeting educational needs

Meeting your educational needs is actually the easy bit, it just requires the discipline and commitment. Accessing the resources you need has never been easier — long gone are the days of trawling through Index Medicus in the local medical library.

When it comes to looking up a topic you have identified as a learning need, there are a few key resources. The vast majority of questions devised for the AKT will be based on information from a handful of sources:

- The *BMJ*
- *Clinical Evidence*
- The *BNF* and other resources already discussed above

We have already discussed the *BMJ*, but there are a couple of other points to make about using it to look up a topic. You can simply use the website search facility but the problem then is that quite often it returns too many results. Check to see if what you are interested in has been the subject of a themed issue, an ABC series or an *Education and Debate* article. The journal also has a section of collected resources where articles are grouped according to subject area (for example diabetes, coronary heart disease), which can make life much easier.

*Clinical Evidence* is another publication by the *BMJ* group and appears in a book about the same size as the BNF as well as on the website. The advantage of the website is that it is always up to date and it is searchable. You should be able to gain full access to the website via your NHS intranet connection; it is available by subscription otherwise. *Clinical Evidence* is the definitive resource for many of the clinical questions and takes the form of systematic reviews of the topics covered. It is not completely comprehensive and a lot of its content is not directly relevant to GPs, so use it to look things up rather than as a book to browse.

*Bandolier* is another useful resource, published by the Oxford Centre for Evidence Based Medicine. Again the website is easy to use with a good search facility.

*GP Notebook* is a popular resource for both doctors and patients. It is user friendly and is easy to read, and the information given is also referenced. As its name suggests it is really aimed at general practice and most searches deliver highly relevant content. Its ease of use makes it ideal for looking things up quickly between patients — or even with the patient there.

### 3.5.4 Practice questions

It is always helpful when preparing for a multiple choice examination to practice past papers. However times change and there are reasons why this might not be as helpful as it used to be.

There are many books of practice questions for the nMRCGP, and some of these seem to reappearing re-badged as AKT practice questions which is probably reasonable enough since they are mosly from the same question bank. There is also websites offering practice questions. Authors write these questions generally in one of two ways. The first method is to actually create the questions themselves, the second is to recreate questions from live exams by offering candidates incentives to recall questions after they have sat the exam. This method has the disadvantage that the authors do not generally have the expertise of the group of authors who write the genuine questions, nor do they have the psychometric backup and experience required to construct question that are valid and reliable while offering the appropriate degree of difficulty (we will discuss features that affect the degree of difficulty in the next section).

The second method, recreating question,s causes different problems. To avoid copyright infringement authors have to change the wording slightly, which can completely change the integrity of a question. In a situation such as this it gives the College a bit of a headache as it wishes to maintain the secrecy of its question bank. This is even more the case now that the AKT is part of a licensing examination. Of course the examiners know which questions have been compromised so they are likely to be removed from the question bank. Practising these questions does have its usefulness but you aren't likely to see any of them in the live exam.

So what is the benefit of practice questions? The main benefit is that you get to test your knowledge in the areas that the exam covers. You also gain experience with the various question formats. You can also get an idea of how quickly or slowly you can answer the questions. To some extent, possibly more so with the questions taken from the exam, you can get an idea of how well you are doing. Do remember though that a lot of effort has been put in over the last 20 years to develop the MRCGP multiple choice questions to ensure that they really do test your knowledge and to reduce the extent to which you can hone your *exam technique* by deducing the correct answers from the wording of the question.

## 3.6 How to maximise your performance on the day

### 3.6.1 Getting there on time and in the right frame of mind

You have been preparing for months, reading the *BMJ*, practicing questions; finally the big day arrives. It is very important to get it right on the day, so this section will discuss how you can try to ensure that you perform at your best.

First consider the day before — it may sounds really obvious but make sure you give yourself a chance by not turning up tired. It is unlikely in this day and age that you will be on call the night before the exam, but try to relax and make sure you get enough sleep. You will not improve your performance by burning the midnight oil reading journals. It might be worth glancing through any revision notes you have made but do not sit reading all evening. Similarly having a big party night probably is not such a good idea.

Do something that will relax you and take your mind off the exam, that might mean spending time with family or some friends, going to the cinema, maybe some exercise. Do not spend it with friends who are also doing the exam the next day as the conversation will inevitably focus on the exam, and some bright spark will manage to mention all the things you do not think you have covered enough at or some important paper you have never heard of.

Make sure you know exactly where you are going and allow enough time to travel. Roads can get very congested and a minor accident tends to cause interminable delays. If you are driving make sure you know where to park. It is tempting to travel with friends, but if you do, make sure they are not going to make you late and ensure you agree to leave at a time you are comfortable with. Make a contingency plan in case there is a problem, for example a car not starting. If something does delay you try not to panic as there are some things that are completely outside your control and if something goes wrong you must try to stay calm and be constructive about it. There is no point arriving at the exam centre 20 minutes late with your blood pressure through the roof and your brain fried. If you are late you must just try to focus and do your best when you get there.

One of the disadvantages of lift-sharing is again the issue of talking about the exam — it inevitably makes you more nervous rather than less. Try to find something else to talk about, for example football, your trainer's latest awful tie, anything rather than the exam.

The exam centre is likely to be a fairly comfortable environment. In any case make sure you are dressed comfortably with layers you can add/remove.

When you get to the centre you will need to prove you are who you say you are by producing photo identification. There will be a quarantine system to prevent candidates sitting the exam in the morning communicating with those sitting in the afternoon. The implications of this are that if you are sitting in the morning you will not be allowed to leave early, and if you are sitting in the afternoon you will be allowed in if you arrive late.

When you arrive you will not be allowed to take anything into the examination room with you, that includes writing implements, mobile phones or other electronic devices and food/drink. Water will be provided for you and you will be given an erasable note board for jotting notes which will then be retained in the room. You can also jot notes electronically on a scratch-pad facility on the computer.

Using the computer should not be an issue as it is likely you use a computer every day of the week. If you have any problems ask the staff for help as that is what they are there for. You can access a tutorial on the Pearson Vue website and I strongly recommend that you have a go at this at least once before you take the exam.

When you get into the centre you will be able to complete a 10 minute tutorial with sample MRCGP questions before you start the real exam. Answering the questions is simple, you just click on the button next to your chosen answer, the letter next to it (i.e. A, B, C etc.) or on the actual text of the answer. You can also choose an option via the appropriate letter on the computer keyboard.

Before you start answering the questions make sure you read the instructions provided. These will include a brief glossary of terms such as *in the majority, in the minority, has been shown, recognised* and *reported*; make sure you understand these and any other instructions before you proceed.

### 3.6.2 Answering the questions

Make sure you read the questions carefully. Take the questions at face value and trust the examiners as a lot of effort has been put into making the questions as clear, unambiguous and fair as is possible. Do not look for hidden meanings and trick questions as there genuinely are not any.

There will be a huge range of questions, not only in the areas they are testing, but also in the degree of difficulty. Of course if you know the answer any question is easy, but there will be some questions that will be genuinely difficult. Similarly there will be some that look easy. The difficult questions are there to discriminate between the high-flying candidates and inevitably you will come across some questions where you really have not got a clue. Do not panic, read the question carefully and apply some of the strategies outlined below.

If you read the question and know the answer straight away without even looking through the options just double check through the options to make sure you are not missing something, then record your answer and move on to the next question. Excellent, you just scored an easy mark!

However for the majority of the questions you will need to apply more thought. Maybe there are a couple of the options that you think might be correct, in which case concentrate on those to see which you think the more likely. Maybe there are a couple of the options that you know are wrong, in which case you can narrow your odds down a bit. Occasionally there are words in the options that can help you, such as *never* or *always* — it is rare in medicine for something to be always or never true. However the examiners know these words give you clues so will try to avoid using them in the questions.

Once you have excluded what you can — if you really are not sure — and what you cannot choose between the remaining options, you will need to guess. Whatever you do, **do not fail to answer a question**, you really must have a guess or you are wasting a chance of a mark. Be aware that even when you are not sure your guesses are not random, they may be informed by partial recall of something you have read in the past. You have the choice of either leaving the question and coming back to it or committing yourself to a guess straight away. Deferring your answer has the advantage that when you come back it might appear clearer or you might have remember something useful. If you guess you can still go back and change your answer later if you like.

Do not be disheartened by the questions you do not know, the chances are if you are sitting there thinking a particular question is difficult most of your fellow sufferers will be thinking the same. You know before you go in there that you are never going to get 100%, so give each question your best shot then move on without getting upset about it. Just make sure you attempt each question with a clear head as worrying about the previous question will only impair your performance.

Keep an eye on the time — the computer screen will continuously display the time remaining. Most people have enough time to complete the exam comfortably, but you will not finish as early as you might have in the past with the older format of multiple true/false answers.

Once you have finished check to make sure you have answered all the questions. Some candidates prefer to go through some of the questions they were less sure about again, whilst others prefer to have one first try at them and not go back. This is down to your own personality, but generally speaking going back changing answers is not a good idea unless you really have remembered something new as there is a risk you change a correct guess into a wrong guess as well as vice-versa.

If you want to leave a question until later you can as it is easy enough to revisit your unanswered questions at the end of the exam. You can also answer it but select a *review* checkbox and go on to the next question. When you get to the end of the exam the software will present you with a list of all the questions you have either marked for review or not completed. Bear in mind that you must complete all the questions within the time allowed for the exam, as at the end of the allocated time the screen will go blank and you will not be able to answer any further questions.

Once you think you have finished it is best to leave. Do not fill the time just going over the questions again, as it just leads to increased anxiety levels as you start to doubt some of the answers you were previously happy with. Remember though that if you are sitting in the morning session you will not be allowed to leave early.

Once you leave it is best to have something planned to occupy your mind. It is usual to chat with friends about the exam and no doubt this is what you have done before, but ask yourself if the post-exam dissections ever make you feel better about your performance. The answer is invariably no and the focus is inevitably on the more memorable questions which are usually the ones you all found very difficult.

Go shopping and treat yourself, spend some time with your family or friends — do something positive that you enjoy and put the exam behind you. There will be plenty of time to reflect and dissect the paper at your leisure later.

### References

Eve R (2003) *PUNs and DENs: Discovering Learning Needs in General Practice.* Radcliffe Publishing, London

Lewis S, Clarke M (2001) Forest plots: trying to see the wood and the trees. BMJ 322: 1479-80

**Resources**

**Bandolier**: www.jr2.ox.ac.uk/bandolier

**British Hypertension Society**: www.bhsoc.org

*British Medical Journal* (BMJ) www.bmj.com

*British National Formulary* (BNF): www.bnf.org

**British Thoracic Society**: www.brit-thoracic.org.uk

*Clinical Evidence*: www.clinicalevidence.com

**Control of Substances Hazardous to Health**: www.hse.gov.uk/coshh/index.htm

**Data Protection Act 1998**: www.opsi.gov.uk/ACTS/acts1998/19980029.htm

**Driver and Vehicle Licensing Authority** (DVLA): www.dvla.org.uk

**European Computer Driving Licence**: www.ecdl.nhs.uk

**GMS contract**: www.opsi.gov.uk/si/si2004/20040291.htm

**GP Notebook**: www.gpnotebook.co.uk

*Lancet*: www.thelancet.com

**National Institute for Clinical Excellence** (NICE): www.nice.org.uk

**Pearson Vue**: www.pearsonvue.com

**Royal College of General Practitioners** (RCGP): www.rcgp.org.uk

**Scottish Intercollegiate Guidelines Network** (SIGN): www.sign.ac.uk

**UK Resuscitation Council**: www.resus.org.uk

# Chapter 4

# The Workplace Based Assessment

The Workplace Based Assessment (WPBA) essentially replaces the structured trainer's report. There are several reasons why this component is required, the most important probably being that it assesses competency areas that cannot reliably be assessed in the other parts of the exam. There are important aspects to being a doctor that require more than just a snapshot assessment as can be delivered via the AKT and the CSA, such as professional values and teamwork.

There are quite a few elements of the WPBA that are more concerned with formative assessment that the summative process of deciding whether you pass or fail. Formative assessment refers to an assessment that is used for the benefit of the learner, usually in the form of structured feedback, while summative assessment refers to an assessment that has a pass or fail decision attached to it. This handbook will attempt to focus mainly on those aspects which pose a potential threat to overall success in the exam, although some coverage will be given to the remainder.

It is somewhat unusual to combine formative and summative elements within the same assessment, the major concern raised being that if the learner knows his trainer is making a judgement as to his performance he will be less likely to own up to his weaknesses. The counter argument to this is that the distinction is somewhat artificial, as GP trainers have always completed a trainer's report which is essentially summative in nature.

## 4.1 The competency areas

The College has defined 12 competency areas for WPBA. They are listed below but a detailed discussion of each will be provided as there is plenty of information about them on the College website:

- Communication and consultation skills
- Practising holistically
- Data gathering and interpretation
- Making a diagnosis/making decisions

- Clinical management
- Managing medical complexity
- Primary care administration and information management and technology
- Working with colleagues and in teams
- Community orientation
- Maintaining performance, learning and teaching
- Maintaining an ethical approach to practise
- Fitness to practise

## 4.2 The educational supervisor

One significant change in this system of assessment has slipped through rather quietly — that is the introduction of an educational supervisor to provide continuity throughout the training in hospital posts. Previously a trainee who had four six-month posts would have four consultants who would be both clinical and educational supervisors. Although arrangements are likely to differ around the UK it is likely that the vast majority of those in specialty training for general practice will have a GP trainer as their educational supervisor during their hospital posts, and in some areas this may well be the trainer they will be with in their general practice placement. Naturally the trainer in their training practice will take over as both educational and clinical supervisor during the general practice attachment.

The consultant acting as clinical supervisor will retain responsibility for carrying out the various assessments detailed in this chapter, but the trainer acting as educational supervisor will be responsible for providing an overview, working with the trainee to develop a learning plan, make sure their portfolio develops appropriately, ensure that they engage with their clinical supervisor and that the various assessments take place. He will also be responsible for the clinical supervisor's reports.

## 4.3 What the WPBA is designed to assess

The issue of professional values — this encompasses all the attitude aspects of being a doctor:

- Caring and compassion
- Honesty
- Self-awareness and attitude to being a lifelong learner
- Motivation and ability to work within a complex team

A good GP trainer will always have a good idea of how well his or her registrar is performing, and much of this impression is formed based on the informal observation of multiple sources of data: entries in records, informal comments by patients and staff, engaging in tutorials and of course by direct observation of the consultation, usually achieved by watching video recordings. The goal is for WPBA to make these assessments much more explicit and much more objective. This chapter will explore the various tools developed for this purpose:

- Multi-source feedback (MSF)
- Patient satisfaction questionnaire (PSQ)
- Consultation observation tool (COT)
- Case based discussion(CbD)
- Direct observation of procedural skills (DOPS)
- Mini-clinical evaluation exercise (CEX)
- Clinical supervisor's report (CSR)

The evidence gathered for the WPBA throughout training as well as through outcomes from the AKT and CSA, is to be recorded in a web-based portfolio. The ePortfolio can be accessed by the registrar and the educational supervisor who will both be able to make entries in appropriate areas within it. Evidence from external assessments will also be recorded and the WBPA will not be able to be signed off until the AKT and CSA have been passed.

## 4.4 Multi-source feedback (MSF)

Multi-source feedback enables the gathering of views about a registrar from several colleagues. The process is scheduled to take place twice in Specialty Training Year 1 (ST1) and twice again in Year 3 (ST3 — the year in general practice).

During each MSF you will need to select five colleagues with whom you work and ask them to complete an online questionnaire about you. Your trainer will be responsible for ensuring that the sample of colleagues did contribute to it, but he or she will not be aware of the raw responses.

Once complete the results will be sent to the trainer for debriefing. The results will be in the form of mean, median and range of scores for the rating scales and the anonymised free text feedback.

The questionnaire consists only of two questions asking for an overall rating of the registrar's overall professional behaviour and clinical performance, along with space for free text comments both positive and negative.

Your trainer and you will discuss the results of the questionnaires in a meeting and any reflections based on this will be recorded in the ePortfolio learning log.

As such you cannot actually fail MSF, but any serious concerns could result in a referral to more senior Deanery personnel. Serious concerns could arise either as a result of adverse scores and comments in the feedback or of a failure to respond positively to the discussion with the trainer. Both of these should be easy enough to avoid by reviewing the wording of the questionnaire forms (available to download from the College website) at an early stage in training and by considering the appropriate behaviour to elicit positive responses. It may be helpful to ask your trainer for informal feedback on a regular basis.

Similarly, the discussion with the trainer need not be a cause for concern; if there are any issues raised by the questionnaire your trainer will work with you to identify strategies to improve your performance and skills.

A little self-awareness is important when selecting the respondents. Throughout your training you should always try to gauge how others feel about you and respond to you, and it would be wise to apply some careful thought as to whom you invite to complete your feedback questionnaires.

## 4.5 Patient satisfaction questionnaire (PSQ)

Forms will be handed out on an agreed date to consecutive patients. The forms are anonymous and the patients do not give out any clinical information about themselves or their medical history. Patients will complete these questionnaires after the consultation and hand them back at reception. This continues daily until 40 patients have responded. The responses are then entered online — who does this remains undecided as quite reasonably it has been pointed out that allowing the registrar or trainer to enter them leaves the opportunity for false results to be entered. Even if these are entered independently there are still significant questions to be asked of this process as it is not blind.

After completion of all the questionnaires there will be a similar feedback interview with the trainer as in MSF.

To generate serious concerns in the PSQ should surely require considerable effort! The actual feedback forms are not available at the time of writing but since you will know exactly when patients are completing the questionnaires it should not be difficult to ensure you 'tick the right boxes' when you see them — being polite and a good listener will go a long way, but do not lose sight of the fact that most PSQs include an element of the patient assessing your clinical doctoring skills.

## 4.6 The consultation observation tool (COT)

The expectation is that a trainer will assess 12 of your consultations over the course of your year in practice. Consultations can be assessed by live observation but most are expected to be video recordings.

The trainer will assess each consultation according to the COT performance criteria. These criteria are very closely aligned to the old MRCGP video criteria which is good news as it means that even if you have never met them before your trainer probably knows them quite well. The criteria cover five different areas within the consultation:

- Discovering the reasons for the patient's attendance
- Defining the clinical problem
- Explaining the problem to the patient
- Addressing the patient's problem
- Making effective use of the consultation

Your trainer will use these criteria to form an overall judgement on you consultation. The following grades will be used:

- Excellent
- Competent
- Needs further development
- Insufficient evidence

The trainer is expected to record feedback and recommendations for further development, and at the interview when the consultation is discussed you are expected to agree an action plan for improvement.

There has been considerable discussion about the fact that your own trainer will be making this assessment, but working out a feasible methodology for external assessment has been fraught with problems. It is currently recommended that at least one other assessor (another trainer or course organiser or programme director) is involved in rating a few of the cases.

Again this is not a tool expected to 'fail' registrars; it is intended to give feedback and specific pointers towards improvement. The key will be in ensuring that the grades demonstrate improvement during the year from 'needs further development' towards 'excellent' nearer the end of the year.

However, a very important point is that although the COT is not going to be perceived as a terribly high hurdle, the CSA will probably be considered by most to be the most challenging part of the nMRCGP. It is very important that you gain all you can from the formative feedback you receive during the COT process since this will prepare you for the CSA. The marking criteria for the CSA are quite different from the COT but the same principles of patient centred consulting are involved. For that reason we will explore the COT criteria a little further, although there will be more discussion of consulting techniques in the CSA chapter. The College website has a detailed guide to the performance criteria so the following section will be a relatively simple guide.

One important suggestion to make at the beginning is that there are pitfalls in using the 'consulting-by-numbers' approach of trying to attain the performance criteria individually without paying regard to the overall intention of what you are supposed to be achieving, namely that you end up with a dysfunctional, unnatural feeling consultation that appears to registrar, trainer and patient alike as being stilted and wooden. A good consultation can achieve the criteria while still having a natural flow. It may be helpful to think carefully about the five main headings as well as the individual criteria since they convey what they criteria are supposed to be achieving.

Make sure you use your trainer as a resource during your teaching sessions and indeed in the video feedback sessions using the COT. Make sure you ask how your trainer would have done something if you do not think you did it well. Do not be put off asking to sit in with your trainer and watch some of his consultations. All registrars sit in with their trainer during the very early part of their time in the practice, but you are in a position to be aware of so much more of what is going on in the consultation when you have more experience.

- *Discovering the reasons for the patient's attendance*

This is all about finding out why the patient came to the surgery and what their ideas, concerns and expectations are. It requires active listening skills and the ability to be able to encourage the patient adequately without interrupting. Some of the information may be conveyed non-verbally, so you need to be on the lookout for facial expressions, body language, pauses and have the ability to apply your own non-verbal skills to explore the patient's agenda. This includes putting the patient's problem into a social and psychological context, which is beyond asking what they do for a living or who lives at home with them. You need to demonstrate genuine interest and really try to find out what is going on inside the patient's head, what makes them tick.

During junior hospital jobs young doctors tend to develop bad habits that are hard to break later. You will need to concentrate on trying to only ask open questions (during the early part of the consultation at least) and not interrupting the patient. As doctors we are worried that if we just let the patient talk they will go on for ever, but this is not usually the case. Try it yourself and see; you will generally find they run out of steam after a minute or two, and some patients will actually get uncomfortable doing all the talking and will want you to contribute.

It can be disheartening as a registrar to keep asking patients what they think might be wrong only to get very non-committal answers at best or *'you're the doctor' at worst!* You need to ask yourself why it is that patients are not prepared to own up to what they are worried about and think about how you can address that. Generally speaking, patients are acutely aware that you know far more medicine than they do and are therefore afraid of appearing silly if their ideas are off the mark, or are afraid you will think they are hypochondriac and/or neurotic. Therefore when you asking what they thought the problem might be they shrug and say they do not know, then when you tell them what you think it is they say *'yes, I thought it might be that'*!

The trick here is to get the patient to trust you, and there is no simple form of words can be offered as suggestions, it is important that you develop your own ways of achieving this based on your own personality and style. Very often you can second guess what the patient is worried about, for example and without generalising, patients with headaches are often worried about brain tumours and strokes, patients with chest pain heart attacks and blood clots etc. You can utilise this by speculating out loud, for instance: *'I wondered if you had any worries that it might be something serious like a brain tumour'*, or *'people with these sort of symptoms are often worried it might be their heart ...'*. Experiment and find phrases that you feel comfortable with, trying not to make it sound formulaic, as if it feels uncomfortable to you it probably will to the patient and you will get nowhere.

Remember here that this is not just about surviving an assessment, it is about being a good doctor. Remember that one of the commonest things patients say about a doctor they like is he really listens to you. Being a popular doctor is not the be all and end all, but it is very rewarding when patients like you and come back to see you for the right reasons.

- *Defining the clinical problem*

This is about attempting to make an accurate diagnosis. To do this you need to make appropriate hypotheses about differential diagnoses and ask the right questions to include/exclude likely conditions, followed by an appropriate examination. Experience with the MRCGP video examination has led to concerns that some registrars concentrate on the communication aspects of the consultation to the detriment of the practical clinical skills and decision-making.

One of the problems registrars run into is that they are not sure when to stop using silence, listening and using open questions and when to take charge of the consultation and get on with the more closed medical questions. The consultation then ends up a bit disorganised and loses focus.

Sometimes it can be helpful to flag up specifically to the patient that you are going to move into a different phase of the consultation. Once you are happy that you have gathered enough information regarding the patient's concerns it can be helpful to reflect back to them your interpretation of the reason they came. For example you might say something like: *'Just to be sure I have understood correctly, you have come about these headaches you have been having in the evenings, and you were worried they might be due to something serious?'*.

Once you have ascertained that you have understood correctly you can indicate that you are going to take charge a bit more, saying something like: *'I would like to ask you a series of questions now about your symptoms'*.

When you come to examine the patient get into the habit of asking permission and explaining what you want to do and why in plain language, for example: *'Would it be OK if I popped you onto the couch so I can feel your stomach?'*.

It is particularly important that you flag up any aspects of the examination that might be uncomfortable or which might be misinterpreted, even a simple examination like fundoscopy can appear odd to a patient if they do not know what to expect or why you are doing it. Remember also to ask the patient if they would like a chaperone, especially if you are examining women or children

Use some common sense in deciding if an examination is adequate to be seen on camera. Clearly an intimate examination such as a breast examination must be off camera, either out of shot or by covering the lens, but not every exposure of flesh requires this. If you cover the lens for simple examinations, for example examining a child's chest or looking into their ears, your trainer or external assessor is going to be worried about what you are trying to hide! If you are not sure about your examination technique then ask your trainer for some help with it rather than trying to conceal your weaknesses. Just make sure you conduct a clinically appropriate examination.

Remember that you are training to be a GP, not a neurologist, so choose a focused examination that is likely to help you in your decision-making and/or reassure the patient that you have examined them satisfactorily. This is not your medical student finals so you are not generally expected to conduct a full cardiovascular examination or a full neurological examination (unless it is really appropriate). Do however use the correct techniques for the examination you do carry out, and do not do silly things such as listening to a child's chest through a duffle coat!

Remember that the assessor cannot make a judgement about the appropriateness of your diagnosis unless you make it clear what that is. You can also of course record your working diagnosis in the consultation log.

- *Explaining the problem to the patient*

Make sure the patient understands your explanation, the commonest problem here is the use of medical jargon, and you will almost always find you are using more than you think you are. The only way you are likely to pick this up is by watching yourself on video and looking for it specifically. One of the problems again is that patients do not want to appear stupid. So when you say, for example: '*I can see some conjunctival erythema*', they are likely to nod sagely and pretend they understand exactly what you are talking about when they may in fact not have a clue.

'*The white of your eye looks a bit red*' is more user friendly and conveys just the same information.

At this point it gets you even more brownie points if you refer back to the patient's health ideas in your explanation. Apart from impressing your trainer it makes the patient feel like you have listened to them and care about their concerns. This is not terribly difficult, you just need to get into the habit of doing it and it is well worthwhile as you will find you achieve more in your consultations.

• *Addressing patient's understanding*

You need to make sure the patient has understood your explanation. This is difficult to do well at first, until you find effective ways of doing it. Certainly just simply asking if the patient has understood will not suffice as they will generally collude with you to make you happy, and asking them outright to explain the problem back to you really does not work well as it makes the vast majority of patients feel very uncomfortable — if you have never watched this done on video you do not need to look too carefully to see the expression on the patient's face, they often visibly squirm in their seat. Think through the problem here; patients do not like admitting they have not understood your explanation as they do not want to appear stupid themselves and also they do not want to offend you by suggesting that your explanation was incomprehensible!

Experiment with different techniques and avoid formulaic phrases, for example: '*What are you going to tell your wife when you get home?*'. Although this can work if done well, it often results in the patient looking at you as if you have just landed from Mars.

It can help to suggest that what you explained was a bit complicated and difficult to understand and offer to clarify any bits they did not quite get, or even to suggest that sometimes you find it difficult to explain the problem clearly and that you would be happy to go over it again. This will help the patient feel it is not their fault they did not understand and will make them more inclined to ask for clarification.

• *Involving the patient*

You are also expected to come up with an appropriate management plan and to involve the patient in the decision-making process. Make sure your management plan is medically appropriate and that if you are challenged you can justify any investigations, prescriptions or referral, by reference to evidence and guidelines if possible. As a GP in training there is an understandable emphasis on patient safety.

Involving the patient is something you need to start practicing early on as it is something you are unlikely to have done in your hospital posts. Again do not just think of it as something to do to keep your trainer happy as it is a genuinely useful tool to be able to use in the consultation — it means your patient is more likely to leave the consulting room happy and more likely to comply with whatever management plan you have agreed. It needs to be done selectively, and there will be times when it is appropriate to be fairly doctor-centred and directive, for example when you suspect the patient has a serious condition, but it is usually still possible to involve them in the decision-making to some extent. It is important also not to start offering the patient options that are inappropriate, for example antibiotics for a simple uncomplicated cold.

There are lots of occasions when the way forward is not clear-cut and where more than one approach can be justified — many would argue that this applies to most problems in general practice.

The threshold at which you either wait and see or treat/refer is rarely black and white and the patient's opinion can usefully be taken into consideration. Some patients really do not like investigations or taking tablets while others would like to intervene early. If you are not certain what to do it can be helpful explaining this to the patient, they may have a view that helps make the decision easier.

Involving the patient in the management decision does not necessarily mean doing what they want, there are many other factors to take into account, such as our responsibility to other patients and to use resources sensibly. Nor does it mean abdicating your responsibility to the patient — if there is a difficult decision it is your responsibility to help the patient to inform that decision but if the patient wants to leave it to you as a health professional that is their right.

* *Making effective use of the consultation*

You are expected to make effective use of your time and of the patient's. Practice being efficient, recognising when you have enough information to move the consultation forward, asking focused questions rather than wasting time asking lots of questions which do not actually contribute to the decision-making process.

When you think you have done enough you should be able to close the consultation efficiently but politely. Make sure it is clear to the patient if and when they should come back — you do not always need to be very specific but sometimes it is helpful to give conditional instructions, for example suggesting you will review the patient in a month but earlier if there are any problems.

## 4.7 Case based discussion (CbD)

This tool is designed for use during both the hospital and practice based components of training. The idea is that the trainee documents a case which is then used as the basis for an interview with the trainer/supervisor. The purpose is to explore professional judgement in situations of complexity and uncertainty, applying medical knowledge, ethical and legal frameworks and prioritising appropriately. Justification of decision-making will be sought.

To make things easy the trainee chooses a selection of cases for discussion, although the assessor will decide which ones to discuss. There are to be six discussions during each training year for ST1 and ST2, with 12 in your general practice year. The case paperwork has to be made available to the assessor beforehand so he can plan questions he wishes to ask. There are bo specific criteria as to which cases the trainer should choose, but trainers are likely to choose cases that look like they have more scope for discussion, so it is likely to be the more complex cases or ones where the trainer felt perhaps that you could have handled the case differently.

The CbD paperwork is all downloadable from the College website, including the guidance to trainers on formulating structured questions. Again the CbD is not something you can actually 'fail' although the interviews will contribute towards the final WPBA assessment. Remember that WPBA is largely about formative assessment, so the discussions are a learning experience with some assessment thrown in. Good case-based discussions can be challenging and really make you think.

First of all you need to select your cases. It is probably best not to go for completely straightforward cases as there will be little to discuss and you will get nothing out of the process, not to mention the fact that you will get little credit as they will not demonstrate much to the assessor. On the other hand you do not want to select cases you think you made a mess of, unless you are confident you have analysed what went wrong and are confident you can suggest better ways of managing the problem. Very complex cases may not be such a good idea as they can take a lot more than the recommended 20 minutes to discuss, the result then being that you risk having a fairly superficial discussion skating over lots of issues without discussing any in any depth.

When you write up the cases it should be easy enough to work out what issues are likely to come up. Work systematically through the case starting with the history:

- Did you ask all the right questions? Is there anything else you would have liked to ask in retrospect?
- What examination did you choose and why? Did it contribute to making a diagnosis?
- What investigations did you choose and why? What else might you have done and why didn't you choose that? Make sure you consider the evidence base behind your decisions and justification.
- How did you come to your working diagnosis, what else did you consider and what influenced your decision-making process?
- How did you decide on your next management steps? What other options did you have, and can you discuss the implications of each? Try to think of what challenges your trainer could pose to your decisions and how you might justify the decisions you made.
- If you felt you lacked some knowledge that might have helped you how have you addressed this since
- When considering implications think broadly — implications for whom? Consider the implications for the patient, yourself, the practice team, the NHS generally
- Was there any ethical aspect to the case? If so can you tease this out and discuss your decisions in the context of an ethical framework?
- How did you elicit the patient's views? How did you incorporate them into the management plan?
- How did you feel after the consultation: did you find it stressful? If so why and how did you deal with that? How do you think the patient felt leaving the consulting room?

Your experience during the discussion will depend to some extent on your trainer — there is quite a bit of skill required from his point of view and some trainers challenge their registrar more than others. Unless he or she really much cleverer than you there is no reason for anything to come up in the discussion that you have not already thought of, after all you supply the cases and get a chance to prepare them.

It is important that you do not consider CbD just an academic exercise — the skills being tested are really important to you if you are to be a good GP. It is good to get into the mindset of asking yourself the questions above on a regular basis until you are able to incorporate them into your live decision-making processes while you are with a patient. If you can do this it will stand you in good stead when you come to sit the CSA (see later chapter).

## 4.8 Direct observation of procedural skills (DOPS)

DOPS is an assessment of specific clinical skills that you will need to be a GP. They are intended to be carried out throughout the three years of your training, so you might already have completed some or all of them before starting your year in general practice. These are fairly minor assessments and it is not expected that you fail any of them — if one is unsatisfactory it should simply be repeated.

They are listed below. There are six mandatory procedures that all trainees must be observed:

- Breast examination
- Female genital examination
- Prostate examination
- Male genital examination
- Rectal examination
- Cervical cytology

There are also some optional procedures including various minor procedures. It seems likely at the moment that resuscitation will be included with these.

## 4.9 Mini-clinical evaluation exercise (CEX)

Six CEXs per year are to be carried out during hospital posts as an alternative to COT, which often is not possible in the hospital setting. However as this is still very much in the development phase it could be possible that COTs might eventually be done in hospital too.

A CEX is an observed interaction with a patient to assess your clinical skills, attitudes and behaviours. Following the debrief the assessor will provide feedback and during the discussion areas for improvement will be identified and recorded. Each encounter will need to cover a different clinical area.

At the time of writing documentation for this is scant but this again is not expected to be an onerous hurdle. There is very little information from the College on this at the moment, and it is recommended that you ask your trainer and periodically check the Royal College of General Practitioners website (see the Resources section at the end of this chapter)

## 4.10 Clinical supervisor's report (CSR)

Although entitled 'Clinical Supervisor's Report' it seems that these will actually be completed by your educational supervisor — remember in some areas this will be your GP trainer, in others a different GP trainer to the one you will be with for you year in general practice.

Every six months your educational supervisor will need to conduct a review of your progress to date, collating the evidence gathered from the various assessments and complete a report. You can download a copy of the paperwork for this from the College website.

During the review you will complete a self-assessment in addition to the trainer performing an assessment of your progress in the 12 competency areas set out at the beginning of this chapter.

The assessment part of the report has three main areas:

- Knowledge-base relevant to the placement
- Practical skills relevant to the placement
- Professional competencies — which breaks this down into the 12 competency areas

At the end of training the educational supervisor conducts a final review following which he makes a recommendation to the Deanery regarding your competence. There is no self-assessment at this final review and in the final review the educational supervisor must 'grade' each of the 12 competency areas, the grades available being 'insufficient evidence', 'needs further development', 'competent', or 'excellent'. The form can be viewed at the RCGP website and it is essentially a tick box section.

If the trainer feels you are not competent in any area an expert deanery panel will look at the evidence and adjudicate.

## 4.11 The ePortfolio

The concept of using an educational portfolio in medicine is not new, indeed they have been in use in postgraduate general practice for well over a decade.

The term portfolio in this context derives from the world of art and design, where a student would over the course of his training collect pieces of his work in a portfolio. This would then be assessed to gain qualifications and would be used as a showcase of work to demonstrate the artist's skills.

Early general practice portfolios arose from doctors recording experiences they had encountered in their workplace that identified a learning need. A key element of the process was the reflection required to tease out the learning needs from the event and deduce an appropriate method of meeting the needs identified.

As the internet developed, so have electronic portfolios. One of the benefits of these is that access control can be implemented to allow various different personnel to access and sometimes contribute to the portfolio, based on secure account authentication. Thus in the case of WPBA the registrar and the trainer can contribute directly to the portfolio while external bodies such as the College and Deaneries can contribute outcomes from external assessments. The final outcome can provide proof of completion to both College and Deanery to provide final certification as a GP.

Please read the following sections in conjunction with the relevant pages on the College website. At the time of writing this handbook the WPBA is in a state of fairly rapid development and although every effort will be made to make the book as up-to-date as possible it is inevitable that the WPBA will continue to develop and the latest information will always be made available on the College website.

## 4.12 How to ensure success

You can see from all these sections that the assessment throughout WPBA is very closely linked to the teaching, much of it occurring in teaching-type sessions. Feedback therefore will be continuous, and you should know at an early stage if you are falling short of the mark in any areas and should be able to work with your trainer to ensure any weaknesses receive special attention to rectify the situation. You will not get to the end of your training to find your trainer unexpectedly finds himself unable to recommend your competence!

To get into general practice specialty training you must have demonstrated sufficient aptitude that your are capable of comfortably passing all the elements of WPBA. The major challenge is to make sure this fairly onerous schedule of assessments gets fitted into your placements. Clearly this will be your responsibility although your trainer will share this with you and will endeavour to keep things on track working in partnership with you. You are going to need the co-operation of the consultants and specialist registrars you work with during your hospital placements, and although your trainer will be there to help with this you need to engage with them throughout your training. Make sure you try your best to 'get on' with all the people you work with and maintain regular communication with your trainer.

The WPBA is not a terribly challenging hurdle from the point of view of degree of academic difficulty, it is more a question of motivation, diligence and application. For most GP registrars the major perceived hurdle will be the CSA — do not lose sight of the fact that there is huge overlap between the competencies you need to demonstrate during WPBA and those required for the CSA.

**Resources**
**Royal College of General Practitioners**: www.rcgp.org.uk

# Chapter 5

# The Clinical Skills Assessment

The Clinical Skills Assessment (CSA) is an entirely new assessment. It shares many features with the old MRCGP simulated surgery component, but there are differences. As has been mentioned previously it is expected that registrars will perceive this to be the most challenging hurdle within the nMRCGP, and it is entirely possible that perception proves to be reality.

As its name suggests, the CSA is a test of clinical skills, and they cannot be taught in a book like this. What this book can do however is give you as full an understanding of the assessment as possible — what it is designed to assess, how it actually works, how the cases are designed, and how you will be assessed.

The range of problems you could face in the CSA is almost infinitesimal, just like the range of cases you might face in a surgery in general practice. However the broader nature of the problems and the competencies required to deal with them is much smaller, and what we can do in this chapter is identify and discuss the many themes arising. This may appear confusing but will hopefully become clearer later on in the chapter!

## 5.1 What it is designed to test

The stated purpose of the CSA is: '...*an assessment of a doctor's ability to integrate and apply appropriate clinical, professional, communication and practical skills in general practice' (Royal College of General Practitioners).* What this means is that it will test your competence in these skills by actually making you demonstrate them in a standardized environment.

The CSA will test your ability to actually apply knowledge in a clinical scenario. The CSA provides a variety of standardised cases so that the degree of challenge is controlled by the assessors rather than by yourself; there is an objective, criterion-referenced marking schedule and the grades are decided by a series of independent, highly trained, experienced assessors. Criterion referencing means that your performance is compared against a predetermined level of competence rather than against other candidates — it does not matter how well or how badly others do, and if you perform well enough you pass.

The CSA is thus about far more than just communication skills. Once you have gathered information about why the patient came to the surgery, you must use this along with your medical knowledge to make appropriate clinical decisions and formulate an appropriate management plan. The information gathering may include a physical examination of the patient. The consultation must be conducted in a patient-centred way, seeking out and acknowledging the patient's own ideas about the problem and potential solutions and involving them in the decision-making. Your *professional values* may come under scrutiny, for instance your ability to recognise ethical dilemmas and resolve them satisfactorily.

As stated on the College website the CSA aims to test you in the following areas:

- Primary care management — recognition and management of common medical conditions in primary care.
- Problem-solving skills — gathering and using data for clinical judgement, choice of examination, investigations and their interpretation. Demonstration of a structured and flexible approach to decision making.
- Comprehensive approach — demonstration of proficiency in the management of co-morbidity and risk.
- Person-centred care — communication with patients and the use of recognised consultation techniques to promote a shared approach to managing problems.
- Attitude aspects — practising ethically with respect for equality and diversity, with accepted professional codes of conduct.
- Clinical practical skills — demonstrating proficiency in performing physical examinations and using diagnostic/therapeutic instruments.

## 5.2 When to sit the CSA

The first thing to discuss is when you are actually going to sit the CSA. Initially there are three planned sittings of the exam, and at the time of writing they are not all fixed yet. There will be a sitting in October 2007 followed by further sittings in February 2008 and in either April 2008 or May 2008, but it is possible there might be continuous sittings from February through to May. There is a balance to be struck here — sit it too early and your chances of failing are much higher, but if you leave it until the last sitting before completing training there is a risk you will fail and be unable to start work as a GP.

The following advice applies assuming your year starts in August 2007 — if you started in February 2007 or some other time, or if you are training part time, you will need to adjust accordingly. If your final year is in general practice I would strongly advise that you do not even consider the October sitting since your chances of passing are slim unless you are some sort of prodigy!

It is tempting to sit in February 2008 so that should you fail you still have the opportunity of resitting in May/June 2008. I think however that becoming proficient in the skills we have detailed in this chapter by February and getting it all into ten minute consultations only halfway through the year is a bit of a tall order and that your chances of passing are significantly higher in the May/June sitting. The failure rate of candidates sitting towards the end of their training is expected to be very low.

Should you fail on your first attempt the cost to resit will be the same whether you take the exam in February or in May/June of 2008. Your chances of passing are however higher later on, so the odds are that it will be cheaper to sit later. Should you fail in the May/June 2008 sitting however there is the added complication that you cannot start work as a GP until you resit and pass, and you would not be able do that until October 2008. You then have the option of seeking funding from your Deanery for additional training (which is the ideal) or simply treading water until October 2008. Circumstances in Deaneries will vary, but the Deanery has already invested a lot of time and money into your training, and they have already given you a form of endorsement via the selection process you underwent to get onto the training scheme in the first place, and they are unlikely to abandon you at this stage. However you should discuss this with both your trainer and your course organiser/programme director.

## 5.3 The format of the exam

The examination is in the form of a simulated surgery — you will sit in a consulting room and see a series of 13 simulated patients. You will have a maximum of ten minutes to consult each patient, with a short break of about two minutes between each consultation and a break halfway through.

You will be provided with a brief patient record which may detail any previous relevant or significant medical history, current medication, perhaps brief records of recent consultations, investigation results or hospital letters. The record will be as brief as possible to avoid burdening you with unnecessary information and is unlikely to fill a single side of A4. You will be able to read the record in the gap between consultations.

At the start of a consultation the patient will knock and enter the room and the consultation will begin exactly as it would in your usual surgery. If you have not finished by the time the ten minutes is up the patient will get up and leave when the buzzer sounds.

### 5.3.1 How the cases are designed

There are several ways simulated patient scenarios can be devised. The first thing to say is that the scenarios are all devised by experienced case writers, all of whom are experienced examiners and GPs. Some have had previous experience in writing cases for the simulated surgery in the old exam, but all have had training in writing cases. Cases are generally written in pairs firstly as it can be a bit isolating sitting on your own writing cases, but mainly because two heads really do work much better than one in all aspects of writing the case — coming up with ideas, spotting possible problems and pitfalls and in refining the actual wording.

One obvious way of writing cases is by drawing from experience; typically a writer might experience an encounter with a patient in which something happened that made it stand out as a suitable case. Generally speaking this would be a consultation that featured a specific challenge. The writer then needs to tease out the specific issues raised by the case and trim out any extraneous features that complicate it.

The next step is to identify what this case would be testing by reference to the Curriculum statements and link it with one or more specific *intended learning outcomes,* or ILOs.

Alternatively, the writer must identify a curriculum statement to write a case for, and then choose specific ILOs. The case writer then needs to consider possible clinical scenarios that would test in that specific area. This technique is useful when the management team identify that a particular area of the curriculum is short of cases.

There are three separate elements to the case writing. The first of these is defining what the case is designed to test and what the case writer expects a registrar to have to do to pass the case. The second part is the role player briefing, which defines clearly the age and sex of the role player, the presenting complaint and quite detailed guidance on how to dress, how to behave and how to release information. The final part is of course the examiner's marking schedule which will specify which domains the case tests and what you are expected to do in each to pass.

Case writers face several challenges. While you clearly do not need to appreciate all the intricacies of writing the cases understanding these challenges can help you prepare for the exam. The most important is probably to make sure that the case feels real, important to both you as the doctor consulting the patient but also to the role-player. For you as the doctor it is important that you feel that the patient sitting in front of you is real, and that the problem they present feels just like the sort of thing you face in your day-to-day surgeries. You must be able to get into consultation mode and forget that it is an examination. For the role-player it is important that they can identify with the case and put themselves completely into role and play it naturally without having to think through it too much as they go along.

It is important to make sure the scenario is sufficiently tightly focused, making sure it tests what it is set out to and that it does not present too many opportunities to wander off down blind alleys that are not relevant to the marking schedule. The case writers also must ensure that the case can be completed in the allocated time, or at least cover most of it within the ten minutes you are allowed. This means avoiding too much complexity, while retaining an appropriate level of challenge — a case that is too straightforward and presents too low a challenge does not discriminate sufficiently between good candidates and weaker ones.

The marking schedule must be meticulous. It is very important that it leads the examiner observing the case to reward the correct consulting behaviour and conversely that it does not reward inappropriate behaviour. It can be difficult to make sure that you cannot get sufficient marks just through a mechanistic history taking and examination.

The cases all have to be piloted before they can be used in a live examination. It is impossible to be certain a case will work as planned; some cases fizzle out quickly and need the level of challenge raising, others prove to be too complex for candidates to handle in ten minutes. Often the role-player briefing needs tweaking to ensure description of symptoms enables the good candidates to make a correct diagnosis or to modify the advice to the role-player on the level of cueing to offer. Sometimes symptoms need to be trimmed to avoid candidates following false leads. Similarly the marking schedule will invariably need some adjustments to reflect the reality of how the consultation actually plays out in reality. The aim is to present you with a patient who presents in as realistic a way as possible and gives you the opportunity to demonstrate your consulting and clinical skills.

## 5.4 What you are likely to meet

Theoretically you could come across any medical problem during your surgery in the CSA. However, there are some constraints that can help you narrow down the range of what to expect.

You will not encounter any of the very simple, straightforward and often trivial problems patients often present us with in our day-to-day surgeries in general practice. Although this would add realism, it would add little in the way of helping the examiners discriminate, and at the end of the day that is what an exam is for, to discriminate between candidates from poor through to excellent. Discrimination is generally perceived to be a bad thing in current society, but in this context of course it is not a bad thing, as long as the discrimination is both reliable and valid.

There are huge limitations on what physical examinations the examiners can expect you to perform in the consultations. One limitation is that it is unreasonable to expect the role-players to undergo intimate examinations, or anything that might be considered uncomfortable or the least bit invasive. This even excludes some apparently simple procedures such as checking blood pressure, for which the GMC have issued specific guidance as to how many times a day it is considered reasonable for this to be done on a patient. Also, because this is a licensing examination it is important that all candidates experience a standardised challenge, so any physical signs must be as near as possible to identical for all candidates. This means that using real patients with physical signs as happens in other exams is a problem so physical signs will need to be either simulated by the role-player (for example simulating pain or tenderness, a restricted range of movement of a joint, etc) or using the sort of models or artificial body parts you may have encountered previously in OSCEs.

Despite a desire on the part of the College (and PMETB) to assess your clinical examination skills, in reality the majority of what you will be assessed on will be your communication skills.

The examiners would also like to present you with urgent medical problems, but again there are significant limitations as to what can reasonably be simulated. For example, they cannot present you with a patient who is short of breath, but it is certainly possible to present you with a patient with acute pain who may require urgent management. You should not assume that because it is a simulation a patient could not possibly require an urgent intervention, such as hospital admission.

There are several different aspects to a consultation and this chapter will deal with these in separate sections. Of course in a consultation lots of these merge together and are not separated out, but for the purpose of teasing out everything that goes on and how you can become better at it, it is helpful to identify them separately. Here are the basic components of a consultation:

- History taking
- Examination (physical or mental)
- Making a diagnosis
- Explaining the diagnosis
- Formulating a management plan

## 5.5 The patients

- *Age*

You will meet a variety of patients of both sexes and with a wide range of ages. You will see less children than in a 'real' surgery though since there are practical difficulties in using children (related to length of working hours and missing school). All the patients you meet will be professional role-players, many but not all of whom may be professional actors.

The role-player's age is generally carefully matched to the suggested age of the patient they will be playing. Sometimes this may just be an age range, for example 40 to 50, but for some roles the age of the patient may be quite critical.

To help address the difficulty of using very young and very elderly role-players the patient's and role-player's age may not always match exactly. For instance a role-player in their late 60s may play an 80 year old, or an older teenager may play a younger role. In these cases a lot of effort will be put into ensuring a performance that makes the age of the patient appear credible using dress, make up, etc.

- *Social class*

As well as age and sex mix, the case writers try to provide a balance of social class, from highly educated and articulate patients through to working class or unemployed and relatively poorly educated patients. Remember however that, generally speaking, trained actors are fairly well educated and are invariably articulate, and while they are good actors and can compensate for this to some extent where required it is fair to say that the majority of patients you will meet in your CSA surgery will be articulate and middle class.

- *Ethnicity*

There will be a mixture in terms of ethnicity, in some cases the patient will happen to be Asian or Afro-Caribbean but their ethnicity will be coincidental to the role. In other cases however the patient's ethnicity or cultural background may be a key feature of the case requiring you to specifically address any issues raised by this.

All the role-players receive training before playing a role in the examination. Currently the role-players are sourced from a single agency that also provides role-players for other medical exams, and most of the role-players are already highly experienced. In addition to 'generic' training for their work with the CSA every role-player will have specific training in the individual role to be played which will involve watching video footage of the role being played in its piloting or in a previous live exam, and rehearsing the role with others playing the same role along with the examiners assigned to the case.

A lot of time is spent ensuring that the role-player not only presents the case accurately to you but also that it is done in a highly standardised way so that it is played in an identical way to every candidate. This means not only using the same form of words but includes the emotional level it is presented at — some roles require the patient's mood to be low, anxious, upset, angry, and minor differences in how this is played can have a major effect on the experience that you as a candidate have. Role-players have to be carefully rehearsed in how they are expected to react to what you as a doctor might do or say in the consultation.

All of this detail is provided to reassure you that you can go into the CSA confident that you will be presented with a series of realistic patients and that they will consult with you in exactly the same way as with the candidate in the next room, the day before and the next week, etc. Their job is to present you with a standardised challenge, to play the case accurately without either unduly helping or hindering you. You can just get on with the job of being as good a doctor as you can during your ten minutes with them without worrying about them tripping you up or misleading you.

## 5.6 The consultation

Dozens of books and hundreds of papers have been published on communication skills, and British general practice probably leads the way in this field. This chapter therefore cannot possibly be a comprehensive guide to communication skills for general practice, but I will try to cover the most important aspects, and try to present it in a way that is particularly relevant to the CSA.

I am not going to suggest you go away and read lots of other books either, but there are a couple of key ones you really must read and be aware of. You should hopefully be aware of them anyway, and they should be in the practice library of any self-respecting training practice.

Some of the earliest published work was written in the 1950s by Michael Balint. He worked with some London based GPs and analysed what was going on in the consultation and published his book titled '*The Doctor, his Patient and the Illness*' (re-printed in 2006). This work was important as it came at a time when general practice had fairly low status and people were just starting to consider the psychology of the doctor-patient relationship. I will not attempt to describe the book in any detail here and it is a fairly weighty tome that does not appeal to many GP registrars, but Balint wrote about the feelings doctors had when they consulted patients and how identifying the way a patient made a doctor feel could be quite important. He also encourage doctors to meet together to discuss these feelings, what they meant and what they could do about them. He also wrote about the fact that a doctor himself could act in the same was a drug — with benefits, side effects and the potential for dependence!

In the 1970s Patrick Byrne and Barrie Long listened to 2,000 audiotaped conversations and identified six stages of the consultation (Byrne and Long, 1976):

- Establishing a relationship
- Identifying the reason the patient came
- Conducting a verbal and/or physical examination
- Doctor and/or patient consider the condition
- Doctor and patient agree on further treatment or investigation
- Doctor closes the consultation

Of note they identified that problems in phases two and four of the list above were most likely to lead to 'dysfunctional consultations'. They also described the terms 'doctor-centred' and 'patient-centred'.

In 1979 Nigel Stott and Robert Havard Davis described the primary care consultation as consisting of four parts (Scott and Davis, 1979):

- Management of presenting problems
- Modification of help-seeking behaviour
- Management of continuing problems
- Opportunistic health promotion

Although nowadays generally considered very doctor-centred, this model does promote holistic care.

*'The Consultation — An Approach to Teaching and Learning"* was written by Pendleton, Schofield, Tate and Havelock (1984). The important concept of 'ideas, concerns and expectation' first appeared in their book. Their book also describes the use of a video recorder to analyse and teach consulting skills and described seven tasks:

- To define the reasons for attendance, including the nature and history of the problem, their aetiology, the patient's ideas, concerns and expectations, the effects of the problems
- To consider other problems: continuing problems at risk factors
- To choose with the patient an appropriate action for each problem
- To achieve a shared understanding of the problems with the patient
- To involve the patient in the management and encourage him to accept appropriate responsibility
- To use time and resources appropriately
- To establish or maintain a relationship with the patient which helps to achieve the other tasks.

*'The Inner Consultation'* by Roger Neighbour et al (2004) describes a five stage process:

- Connecting
- Summarising
- Handing over
- Safety netting
- Housekeeping

Although it is the five stages people remember best there are lots of other important observations in Roger's, book making it important reading for all GP registrars to read.

Finally, *'The Doctor's Communication Handbook'* by Peter Tate (2006) summarises most of what is in the other books, along with plenty of other stuff.

It is very easy to read and is a very practical pragmatic guide to consulting.

It is worth noting that Pendleton, Schofield, Tate, Havelock and Neighbour have all been heavily involved in the MRCGP exam and its development over the years. You can interpret this in different ways but whichever way you look at it the College's exam has always had strong links with the development of 'the consultation'.

### 5.6.1 The greeting

When a patient knocks on your consulting room door do you remain seated, stand until they sit or go over to the door and shake their hand? You probably have an innate style that influences this, and there is not a right or wrong approach. It is likely though that while some patients will welcome a more formal approach this may lead to a more formal doctor patient relationship. There are times when you may want that, but perhaps not always.

The opening part of any consultation is very important — there are so many different ways of doing it. If you have read Roger Neighbour's book *The Inner Consultation* you will know that what a patient says when they first walk into the consulting room and how they deliver it can convey more information than is given in the words alone. In the CSA the role-players are carefully briefed to deliver their opening statement in a highly standardised way. All role-players playing an individual case will therefore use exactly the same form of words. Roger Neighbour describes the *curtain raiser* — a spontaneous and unintended remark made by a patient as they enter the room — and argues that it often tells you a little more about what is going on in the patient's head than the statement they have been rehearsing while in the waiting room. While it is of course entirely possible for the case writers to script this sort of thing into the role-player briefing, in the vast majority of cases the patient will have a simple opening statement telling you why they have come. For example: *'I've been having a pain in my stomach doctor'*, or *'I've been worried about these headaches I've been getting'*.

Have you thought about the effect your greeting has on a patient? Have you tried experimenting with different approaches? There are lots of ways of starting a consultation and each is likely to have a different effect on the patient, even when it is a simulation. A traditional medical approach is to directly ask the patient why they have come, with a statement such as: *"Hello Mrs. Jones, what's been the problem?'*, or *'What can I do for you today?'* or *'How can I help?'*, which can in real consultations save some time as it avoids preamble about the weather. A more open and encouraging approach is to open the consultation with a less direct question or statement, such as: *'How are you today?'*, or *'Hello, I'm Dr. Jones'*, or *'I don't believe we've met before'*. You can even actually say nothing but smile and gesture for the patient to sit down. This allows the patient to say what they have rehearsed without you distracting them and tends to make them feel a little less hurried. In your normal everyday consultation the latter approach is more likely to elicit the *curtain raiser* type of response but in the CSA it probably makes less difference. What is important though is that you experiment with the different styles to observe the different responses they elicit and to establish a technique and form of words that you personally feel comfortable with. If you can open the consultation confidently and smoothly you will feel better about it and the patient will feel better about it and will therefore be more likely to volunteer the information you need more easily.

The examiner sitting in the corner watching is likely to notice too, even if only subconsciously and this is important as we'll see when we discuss the marking later. The consequence of a clumsy and uncomfortable start is that the patient will feel less comfortable and you're likely to have to work much harder to gain the information.

Roger Neighbour's describes five 'checkpoints' in the consultation. The first is 'connecting', meaning that you should establish rapport with the patient. Rapport means establishing a relationship with the patient, empathising with them and establishing mutual trust and respect. It is often difficult to pitch your initial behaviour with a patient since they all tend to have slightly different expectations and values. For some the doctor-patient relationship is a formal one, particularly for elderly patients. Others prefer a much more informal and personal relationship where using the patient's first name would be more appropriate that their surname. One constant is that you need to appear friendly and while some of this is about smiling as you greet it is also hugely dependent on your body language. This can be difficult in an exam situation where you are feeling anxious and tense so it will require some positive effort to try to appear relaxed and welcoming.

The role-players will react to you exactly as a patient would, so making them feel welcome and putting them at ease is important. There is a balance to be struck however, and it is important you do not overdo it and appear over-enthusiastic or excessively cheerful! It is also possible to appear smarmy or patronising and you need to watch yourself on video to judge if you are getting it right.

### 5.6.2 Taking the history

Once the consultation is under way you can get down to the nitty-gritty of finding out why the patient came. As a medical student you will have learned a very structured approach to medical history taking which involves asking lots of closed questions and is very *doctor centred*. As a GP you need to move on from this — that is not to say that you can forget all about what you originally learned, but you certainly will not get through much of a routine history and examination in the ten minutes you are allowed. More importantly however you are also likely to miss out on lots of important information. So as well as developing a more focused technique you must become more *patient centred* to ensure you discover all the psychosocial elements to the problem as well as uncovering any hidden agendas.

A lot of the information can be gained for free, without you putting any effort at all in, and it is important that you maximise this. When patients see a doctor they already have lots of information available to give you and it is important to let them do just that! The first technique is to simply not interrupt the patient. This sounds easy but it is something many doctors find very difficult to actually put into practice. It is easy to understand why this is — we are worried that if we just let them talk they will go on forever, but we just cannot resist butting in and elaborating the details of the first important thing they say. Various studies have looked at this behaviour and the average time before the doctor interrupts the patient is reported at under 20 seconds. Similarly the average time the patient talks before appearing to seek doctor input is reported at about 90 seconds, suggesting that we overestimate the amount of time patients will talk if left to it.

It is quite difficult to change this behaviour, so do not wait until you turn up to the CSA before trying it. You need to practice this in your normal surgeries, preferably while video recording so you can observe how long you can actually go before you intervene and so that you can try to appreciate the value of the information volunteered. It is also important to learn to do this appropriately — if you just sit there saying nothing most patients will feel uncomfortable and will probably clam up. So you need to develop what are known as *active listening skills* and develop a feel for when the patient does want you to respond or take a little more active control of the consultation.

- *Body posture*

Active listening means that while listening you are taking some positive steps to encourage the patient to talk. This is generally in terms of non-verbal communication, although often encouragement is vocalised as *'mmmmm's'*, *'uh-uh's'* etc. If you look disinterested or frankly bored the patient will predictably not take this as encouragement. Posture is important; when interested in what someone has to say we generally lean forward, but you need to appear relaxed at the same time or it can appear a little intimidating. An open posture usually means with hands relaxed in your lap or on the desk rather than with arms folded. Eye contact is important; it is no good gazing off over the patient's shoulder, staring at a computer screen or written records or fiddling with your pen. Make it clear the patient has your undivided attention. We also use more subtle facial expressions to make it clear we are listening carefully; sometimes cocking the head to one side, but perhaps more importantly responding appropriately by nodding, frowning, or raising eyebrows. Again it is important that all this is done in a natural way, and if overdone it can be very destructive! Watch yourself on video, ask for feedback from your trainer or other colleagues, and watch others consult if you get the chance so you can observe for yourself what you think works and what does not.

- *Asking further questions*

Where you do feel the need to ask further questions you should always try to ask open questions rather than closed since this allows the patient more freedom to express themselves. The first principle is to try to avoid asking questions that lead to a 'yes' or 'no' answer. Ensure that your question encourages the patient to give more detail, for example: *'Can you tell me a bit more about the pain?'*, rather than *'Was it a sharp pain?'*. Use the techniques described in the previous paragraph to encourage the patient and make sure you give them time to answer.

- *Using silence*

Using silence is an important consulting technique — it can feel uncomfortable and it is sometimes difficult to resist the urge to break the silence either by rephrasing your question or by asking a different question. Remember that if a patient does not understand your question or cannot think of an answer they will usually say so.

Silence in a patient indicates usually that they are thinking of an answer, and is taking some time either because it is something they feel uncomfortable talking about or because they cannot find the right words to express it. Often the silence will be accompanied by loss of eye contact, the patient often lowering their head. You should keep looking at them so you can resume eye contact when they look up. If you do eventually feel compelled to break the silence there are ways of doing this that can give the patient further encouragement, either verbally by acknowledging their difficulty or non-verbally, by touch for example.

- *Presentation*

Just as in real-life, patients in the CSA may not always present in a straightforward way — they may present you with multiple symptoms or their initial presenting complaint may not actually be the main problem. Patients presenting with a list of symptoms can be challenging to deal with and you need to have strategies for dealing with this.

One approach is to take each item in the list at a time and while this may seem appealing there are drawbacks to it. First you are unlikely to have enough time to work your way through any kind of list in the ten minutes you have with the CSA patient. Second this approach often misses the point — a list of symptoms that appear unconnected to a patient may actually be different manifestations of the same underlying problem (for example a patient presenting with tiredness, low mood, poor concentration and irritability). A useful strategy can be to gather all the symptoms together to see if there is any obvious pattern. It might be worth asking the patient if they think they might be connected.

If the symptoms do not appear connected and it genuinely appears the patient is presenting with multiple different problems then you need to prioritise. Patients do not generally mean to make life difficult for us, and often aren't consciously aware that when they book an appointment with us it's for a finite length of time. They also sometimes underestimate the difficulty of some of the problems they throw at us. It is OK to explain to a patient that you have limited time with them and that you might need to arrange another appointment to deal with some of the problems. This needs to be handled sensitively, avoiding making the patient feel short changed or as if you are fobbing them off. Patients will understand that trying to deal with lots of problems in a single ten minute appointment will mean you cannot really do justice to any of them and will lead to a superficial handling.

There is a risk that a patient may be made to feel stupid if your response comes across in the wrong way; you may not mean to sound like you are saying *'You can't possibly expect me to deal with all that lot in one go!'*, but it can seem like that if you do not get it right. It can sometimes be helpful to 'take the blame' yourself, making it sound like a weakness of your own rather than of the patient.

- *Prioritising the problems*

You must involve the patient in the prioritisation, even though it may be obvious to you which problem should be dealt with first. Saying something such as: *'I think I'll struggle to deal with all those problems properly in one go – was there one in particular that you'd like us to address first?'* might be one approach. Or *'Shall we have a go at dealing with the most important problem and see how we are for time after that?'*.

When it comes to spotting hidden agendas there are lots of strategies you can use. Those who argue that consulting is an art rather than a science would perhaps have you believe that the good doctor has a kind of 'sixth sense' for this sort of thing, and just gets a feeling that there is something more there. Whilst it is difficult to disprove this, it is probably more likely that the good doctor is just more expert at spotting the more subtle clues, generally non-verbal ones. The good doctor is probably also that little bit more suspicious that there could always be something going on in the background and actively seeks clues. It does seem that these skills appear elusive to novice consulters, so do not worry if when you start your year in general practice you do not feel as if you are 'tuning in' to much of the background agendas.

Although there is no substitute for experience it is fair to say that experience alone will not be enough and that you certainly can learn the skills required.

- *Patient-centred consulting*

If you recall back to chapter two patient-centred consulting appears prominently in the curriculum. Being patient-centred is not about doing what the patient wants, it is about really tuning in to the patient, finding out about why they came, what exactly it is about their problem that's worrying them and what sort of solutions they thought you might be able to offer.

The term *"ideas, concerns and expectations"*, often shortened to *ICE*, refers to the fact that patients almost always have their own ideas about what might be wrong with them, the seriousness of their symptoms and their implications and they almost always come with expectations as to what you might be able to do.

Patients pretty much always have their own ideas about what is behind their symptoms, but GP registrars often find it difficult discovering what those ideas and health beliefs are. That is because finding this out *is* difficult!

You may ask patients what they think might be causing their symptoms and more often than not they will simply tell you they have no idea. Then later when you tell them what you think the problem is they will say: *'Yes, I did wonder if it might be that'*.

Why do patients do this? This is more common in patients from the lower socio-economic groups – you often find that the more educated patients are all too willing to tell you exactly what they think the diagnosis is, and possibly even what management they expect too, sometimes all of it in the opening 30 seconds of the consultation. For many patients an encounter with a doctor is not exactly threatening, but they certainly do not feel on an equal footing with you. They are acutely aware that you are a highly trained professional who of course knows far more about medical problems than they do, and as a consequence they are very self-conscious about their ideas and worry about divulging them to you: they may be worried they might be just plain wrong and therefore that you will think they are stupid; they may be concerned that despite their worries you will find that there is nothing seriously wrong and you will therefore consider them neurotic; or they might have a stereotyped view of what a doctor patient relationship should be like and be concerned that you will consider them presumptive for considering a diagnosis.

You will need to learn a few tricks to get patients to spill the beans. The first point is not to ask too bluntly — asking simply *'What do you think it is?'* will almost invariably result in a shrug and a denial. You need to be a little more subtle, and ask a little more indirectly. More open questions can be helpful. Asking something like: *'What have you made of all of this?'*, or *'Do you have any theories about what might be causing it?'* sometimes does the trick since it implies their ideas are more tentative. Another strategy is to ask what their family have made of it — that way it is the family who potentially look stupid or neurotic rather than the patient themselves. Timing can be important: asking during the main history-taking phase of the consultation makes it seem a more important question whereas if you can slip it in as an aside a little later, for instance when they are getting on the examination couch or during the examination it can be disarming and may be more likely to result in a frank answer. Again you tone of voice, facial expression and body language are important and you need the patient to believe that you really do expect them to have some ideas of their own and that you will value and respect those. A plea for help can sometimes be fruitful, for instance: *'It would be really helpful to know what you think about it'*.

Often it is not difficult to second guess what the patient's self-diagnosis might be, or they might even have hinted at it, in which case it is easy to offer something such as: *'Did you wonder if it might be ...?'*. It is often worth a stab in the dark even if you have no idea what they are thinking since it might still provoke them into volunteering some information. A statement such as: *'People very often have a good idea about what's wrong with them'* sometimes helps and they are often right.

- *Identifying concerns*

Identifying concerns is very similar but is subtly different. Early on in his *Doctor's Communication Handbook,* Peter Tate points out that patients invariably think their problem is more serious than you do, and this is always worth remembering. Again asking patients directly about their concerns is not always helpful. Sometimes you can use cues, for example: *'You seem quite worried about it'*. Asking something such as: *'Do you have any particular worries"* implies that you assume they do have worries about their symptoms but invites them to tell you about the most serious concerns they have.

The 'guessing what's in the patient's head' strategy can again be helpful. For example: *'Were you worried the headache might be due to a brain tumour?'*. Another approach is to depersonalise the problem, so you might say: *'Lots of patients with headaches worry that they might have a brain tumour. Did you?'*.

- *Pin-pointing the problem*

Having said all this, it is important that you do not overlook the plain old medical history taking. It is really important that you do ask the right questions about a patient's problem to make an appropriate medical diagnosis. A common pitfall in the simulated surgery has been for candidates to concentrate on the communication skills but failing to make a correct clinical diagnosis. One of the key skills you need to learn is when to 'shift mode' slightly in a consultation. In most consultation there does come a time to move on from the open questions, and move into a more doctor-centred phase where you do ask closed questions to test your diagnostic hypotheses and exclude some of your differentials. It can be helpful to 'signpost' this shift to the patient (and even to the examiner!) by saying something such as: *'OK, I think I've got quite a bit of information to go on. Would you mind if I just asked you a series of questions to help narrow things down a bit?'*.

Occasionally a patient might take advantage of the opportunity to talk freely and carry on talking for what seems forever. Although most have some insight and at some stage will stop, this is not always the case. In these cases you will need to intervene to take control of the consultation. There is not a set time for this and it should be dependent on what the patient's telling you — once you feel the information they are giving you is not actually taking you forwards you will need to consider intervening. This might be because they are going round in circles telling you the same thing repeatedly, or describing repeated occurrences of the same symptoms or going off on tangents without focusing on what they actually came about. There are different ways of dealing with this depending on the circumstances, and initially it can be best to just remain silent, withdrawing the earlier encouragement. If that fails it is probably generally better to deal with it explicitly rather than simply interrupting, for example by using a statement like the one at the end of the previous paragraph. Referring back to something they said earlier and asking for clarification can get things back on track while still valuing their contribution. You might need to acknowledge something else they have brought up and explicitly 'park' it and ask if it is alright to come back to that later once you have dealt with the main problem.

• *Summarising*

Roger Neighbour's second checkpoint is 'summarising', which is a way of checking that you have correctly grasped why the patient came. The principle is that you summarise back to the patient what you think you have got out of them. Again you can signpost this to make it explicit what you are doing. For example say: *'Do you mind if I just check that I've understood correctly?'*.

The actual summary should be kept simple. For example say: *'So the main reason you've come is about the headaches, and you were a bit worried they might be migraine?'*. The benefit of this is that it can actually save you lots of time; it is surprising how often we think we have understood why a patient has come but get it wrong, resulting in a dysfunctional consultation where the patient leaves without you actually having addressed their problem.

### 5.6.3 Examining the patient

Once you have completed your history-taking the next stage of information gathering is generally to examine the patient. As has already been pointed out, the options in terms of presenting you with abnormal physical signs are somewhat limited. However, the examiners can still expect you to conduct a wide variety of clinical examinations. Before considering these there are some key points to remember:

■ Choice of examination
■ Consent
■ Technique

• *Choice of examination*

Taking these in turn, the actual physical examination you choose to conduct is really important. This is an examination about general practice, so whatever you choose to do must be appropriate for a general practice consultation. It must be relevant to the patient's problem, and it must be likely to provide further information to help you make a diagnosis.

There is an important balance to be struck between being 'thorough' and focusing your examination to what is important and what can reasonably be fitted into a ten minute consultation. You really do need to use your time efficiently and effectively, while at the same time satisfying the examiner that your examination is sufficient to assist you with your differential diagnosis. The important skill here is in knowing what actually will help you in your decision-making. For example if a patient presents with a headache you might feel that to be thorough you should conduct a full neurological examination. You know however that you cannot possibly fit that into a normal general practice consultation, but do not worry because the examiner knows that too and will be assessing you as a general practitioner, not as a neurologist. The examiner also knows that depending on the actual history much of it is likely to be completely fruitless and a waste of your time. So perhaps you might focus down to checking the patient's blood pressure along with a few key cranial nerves, certainly including examining the fundi.

Occasionally an examination is conducted more to reassure the patient than because you think it might actually give you meaningful information. This would generally be to acknowledge a patient's presumed or elicited health beliefs. For example we know that a common health belief is that nose bleeds are a manifestation of high blood pressure, and therefore any patient presenting with a nose bleed is likely to expect to have their blood pressure checked. In this circumstance it is entirely reasonable to conduct an examination that may well not contribute particularly to your decision making. It is sometimes reasonable to sensitively address the health belief, for instance by explaining that high blood pressure does not generally cause nose bleeds but that you will check the blood pressure anyway to reassure them. You could argue that thus you are potentially reinforces the health belief, but if you do not do it there is a risk of the patient leaving worried!

Think clearly about why you want to conduct a particular examination — practice doing this in your everyday surgeries, and after you have examined the patient reflect on what if anything it contributed. By the time you examine a patient you will generally have some hypotheses about the diagnosis, or a list of differentials. Your examination should be chosen to not only confirm or refute these hypotheses but also to exclude any possible serious conditions.

If an examination is not really required or if it is an examination the examiner would prefer you did not subject the patient to then either the patient or the examiner will advise you of this. If it is relevant you may be presented with information, giving you some physical signs either verbally or on a card. It is best to behave exactly as you would in a 'real' consultation — if you would like to examine the patient speak to the patient about it; do not ask the examiner or look to the examiner for cues.

For patients with psychological problems you would not generally conduct a physical examination but would instead conduct a mental state examination. Again this should be focused and appropriate to the patient's presenting problem.

• *Consent*

If you do wish to examine the patient, it is important to gain permission first. For the patient to be able to give informed consent they must have an understanding of what you intend to do, so you must start by explaining that you would like to examine them and explain what that examination will entail in terms of which part of their body and what form the examination may take.

Do not forget that something that might be entirely routine to you may be completely alien to a patient. Try to put yourself in the patient's position and imagine what their fears of an examination might be — typically that it will either be embarrassing or that you will hurt them. It is important that you are honest — if an examination will cause an element of pain or discomfort do not tell the patient that it is not going to hurt! You are not likely to be allowed to conduct any intimate examinations within the CSA so embarrassment is not likely to be a factor.

Make sure that you are actually asking the patient if it is OK to examine rather than simply telling them. For example say: *"Would you mind if I had a listen to your chest?"*, or *"Is to OK if we pop you on the examination couch and feel your stomach?"*.

You need to avoid the use of jargon and practice using plain English, this includes anatomical descriptions of where you plan to examine as well as any procedures or instruments you plan to use.

If your patient is a child this introduces a couple of other issues. First, you are dealing with at least two patients, both the child and any parents with them, so you need to make sure both understand what you would like to do and both are happy for you to go ahead. Second, children are likely to have a much lower level of understanding and less experience of medical examinations and any explanation must take account of this. Finally, children tend to be more afraid of doctors and are generally naturally more apprehensive so will need more reassurance that you will not cause them discomfort.

• *Technique*

Once you have gained permission you need to go ahead with your examination. While this should be an examination appropriate for a general practice consultation, this does not mean it can be haphazard! You must have a clear idea of what you are examining and perform the examination in a systematic manner. Remember the general principles you were probably first taught when you were a medical student, and at all times treat the patient with courtesy and respect. Remember that the role-player will be playing this part over 20 times in a day and it is important that they are not hurt or damaged in any way. This may sound obvious but handling the patient in a rough manner is a sure-fire way of alienating them and giving a bad impression to the watching examiner.

The fluency with which you conduct the examination is important. You should be confident and relaxed — it helps both patient and examiner if you look like you know what you are doing rather than hesitating after each stage as you think through what you are going to do next.

The first part of the examination is to make sure you gain adequate exposure of the part you want to examine. For example, for a chest examination you really do need to ask the patient to remove their shirt or top, ditto for a shoulder examination. You will also want to be able to compare with the other side, particularly for a musculoskeletal complaint. There will generally be a pre-defined limit for this and if the patient says they would rather not remove an item of clothing you should not push this. Alternatively the examiner may direct you to examine the patient without removing a specific garment.

You should next attempt to gain as much information as possible without touching. You should inspect quickly for anything obvious but remember that you are not likely to see any rashes, skin lesions, swellings or deformities in the CSA. Although the role-players will not have obvious visible abnormalities, they will be very well rehearsed in demonstrating pain on movement, so they may have a limp or appear in some pain while removing clothing. Similarly they will reproduce a limited range of movement or pain on movement very reliably. If the patient's complaint includes pain ask them to point out the exact location for you. If the complaint is musculoskeletal you should elicit an active range of movements — this should be systematic and include all planes of movement. Remember flexion, extension, adduction, abduction and both internal and external rotation. When examining a limb you must always compare with the other side. You must constantly monitor whether any of the movements are causing the patient pain by asking them to let you know and by watching their face as well as the part you are examining.

You do not need to give the examiner a commentary as you examine, but patients appreciate you explaining what you are looking for and why, and remember that commenting to the patient on any obvious abnormality ensures the examiner also knows you have spotted it!

Before actually laying hands on the patient you should check if there is anywhere that is sore so you can avoid causing pain. Being considerate and gentle is paramount; ask the patient to let you know if anything you are doing is painful. You should palpate gently to identify any tender areas and check for any masses or swellings. In the case of joints you need to check the range of passive movements and look for any joint effusion. Depending on the area you are examining there may be specific manoeuvres to perform. There is a list of specific examination techniques you should revise in section 5.12.1. Again remember to always monitor the patient's face for signs of pain or discomfort.

Percussion and auscultation must be performed as appropriate, but you are unlikely to find any physical signs. It is important however to conduct them in a proficient manner — be systematic, practice your technique so it does not look like you have never done it before. This might sound patronising but you probably are not used to examining patients while being observed and assessed by a senior colleague, and most of us are aware that in our day-to-day practice we slip into bad habits and cut corners. Make sure you listen in the right places and that you look as if you would actually identify any physical signs.

As soon as you have finished examining let the patient know they can dress again as it is embarrassing sitting talking to someone when you are half undressed! Even if you have explained what you are doing as you go along, it is a good idea to summarise your findings to the patient at the end of the examination. Again you need to avoid using medical jargon and offer to explain anything the patient does not understand. We will cover explaining in a little more detail in the next section.

### 5.6.4 Diagnosis

In this section we will cover everything that comes after taking a history and examining the patient — this will include making a diagnosis, explaining to the patient, formulating and negotiating a management plan, prescribing and referral.

* *Making a diagnosis*
It is worth taking a little time to consider how we actually make diagnoses as doctors. Early on in our careers we tended to take a comprehensive history and then examine the patient thoroughly before coming to any conclusions. That is not how experienced doctors do it though, especially in general practice where time is at a premium.

What experienced GPs do is start considering hypotheses the moment the patient comes through the consulting room door. By the time the patient has finished telling their story a GP will generally already have a pretty good idea what is going on, and if they do not already have a tentative diagnosis they will have narrowed their list of differentials down significantly. Their choice of examination will be informed by this and they will focus very much on looking for physical signs that help them confirm their putative diagnosis, differentiate between different diagnoses and exclude any more serious conditions that they consider to be on the horizon.

There tends also to be a difference between the way GPs as generalists make diagnoses compared to their specialist colleagues. As generalists we consider problems in a broad context, integrating the psychological and social aspects with the physical medical ones. While we do still narrow down as we home in on a diagnosis, this done on the basis of probability rather than exclusion and generalists tend to be more tolerant of uncertainty. Generalists tend to make their diagnoses by building up an overall impression based on many different factors, each of which contributes a small part of the information being processed.

An example would be a patient presenting with chest pain: a generalist would assess the problem based on the nature of the pain, the patient's age/sex and other contributory risk factors such as whether the patient was a smoker, obese, had an adverse family history, etc. While it might be possible to completely exclude the pain being cardiac, a generalist who considered it to be a very low probability would be comfortable exploring other options without needing to instigate other investigations such as an ECG or blood tests. A specialist would be more likely to want to collect evidence that provided more concrete proof that it was not cardiac.

The differences in approach has important implications for use of the doctor's time and other expensive resources as well as for the patient in terms of exposure to unpleasant investigations and generation of higher levels of anxiety.

Of course GPs do still often need to arrange further investigations and this applies to the CSA as it does in normal consultations although you generally will not require much in the way of investigations during the exam. If you cannot get a diagnosis without investigating the patient it would generally preclude you from satisfactorily completing a consultation, which would then restrict the domains the case can be marked in.

- *Explaining the diagnosis*

We will discuss explaining things to patients generally in this section since in some of the cases you meet you might well be given the diagnosis in the form of an investigation result or an entry in the patient's clinical record. There are two important principles in explaining things to patients in a patient-centred way:

- ■ Tailoring the explanation to the individual patient
- ■ Checking that the patient has understood your explanation

Tailoring the explanation means not only that you pitch your explanation at an appropriate level for the patient and use language the patient can easily understand, but also that you must take into account their previous knowledge and health beliefs. The starting point should generally be to check what the patient knows already (or thinks they know). This raises the same issues as establishing their thoughts about what might be wrong in the first place, so a direct approach asking something like: *'What do you know about angina?'* might not elicit much, whereas asking: *'Had you heard of angina?'* will generally elicit a positive response, following which you can ask: *'What sort of things had you heard about it?'*.

Much of what you ask and explain the patient will depend on your patient's intellectual and educational level — a question that might be worded appropriately for an unskilled factory worker might appear patronising to a university lecturer. Even so you should avoid making too many assumptions; sometimes an apparently poorly educated patient might surprise you with their knowledge and the converse that highly educated patients may have huge knowledge gaps is also true.

It goes without saying that you should use language your patient can understand and avoid using jargon, but experience of watching GP registrars consulting on video is not terribly reassuring! Unfortunately it seems doctors actually use much more jargon than they think they are using. Watch some videos of yourself consulting with the specific remit of jargon-spotting. Once you become aware of the problem it is not difficult to keep it in mind while consulting and adjust your language accordingly. The reasons doctors use jargon is because often the jargon allows us to define or describe something much more concisely or accurately. Part of the problem lies in the fact that patients do not often give us the right sort of feedback — when we tell them something they do not understand they will often collude and act as if they understand exactly what you mean, generally to avoid making themselves or yourself appear stupid.

Checking that the patient has understood your explanation is probably something you find quite difficult. Certainly it seemed to cause candidates a lot of problems in the MRCGP video. Candidates in the MRCGP video tried two approaches that generally fell flat with the patients and caused the examiners considerable irritation, so are best avoided. The first is to ask the patient to repeat back to you what you have just explained to them. While this approach does sometimes work it more often than not makes the patient feel very uncomfortable and results in a rather dysfunctional consultation. The second is to ask the patient what they are going to tell their husband or wife when they get home. Again, it does sometimes work but it often causes patients consternation as it is not a question they are expecting. They also are not quite sure why you are asking them since it is not obvious to all of them that what you are doing is checking understanding. One of the most amusing responses I have heard was: *'I won't be telling her anything, because it's none of her business'*, which certainly brought home the issue of confidentiality to that candidate!

Sometimes just asking simply: *'Is all that clear to you?'*, or *'Is there any of that you'd like me to go over again?'* can be enough. However in some cases this is simply not going to be enough.

Make it seem as if it is quite natural not to understand everything by making it clear that medical things are quite complex and difficult to understand; also by the same token that they are quite difficult for us to explain clearly. So you might say something such as: *'Most patients find that difficult to understand first time round, would you like me to go over some of it again?'*, or *'I'm aware that's a lot to take in ...'* or, *'There's lots of information there, does it all make sense?'*. You must deliver it in a way that encourages the patient to believe that you really do expect a response. You can make it seem like you think it might be your own fault if they do not understand it by using phrases such as: *'I often find it difficult to get that across clearly, did that make sense to you?'*, or *'I'm not sure I explained that very well...'*.

If what you are explaining really is quite complex, it might be worth breaking it into smaller, more manageable portions and checking understanding as you go along. It is also often helpful to offer to see the patient again to go over any bits they do not understand; of course you cannot see the patient again in the CSA but if the offer is delivered credibly the examiner is likely to give you credit for it.

• *Information leaflets*
Many doctors use information leaflets — many of the clinical software systems incorporate them, or you can use Prodigy. Of course none of these will be available to you during your consultations in the CSA, but you can offer a leaflet to the patient. Do not use leaflets as an alternative to explaining things properly though. It is sometimes helpful to just write the diagnosis down on a piece of paper and suggest the patient look it up for themselves and suggest resources they can use on the internet. Offer to discuss or explain what they find when they come back to see you again.

### 5.6.5 Formulating a management plan

Once you have made a diagnosis and explained it to the patient you need to do something about it. In any consultation you will have various options available to you, and it is important that you think about this carefully. It often works as a sort of cascade, moving from the most minimal interventions through to the more significant ones.

The first option available to you is to **do nothing**. While it can often be applied quite literally, it generally involves doing nothing more than explaining things to the patient or reassuring them and allowing some time.

The next step up the ladder is to actually provide some treatment by **prescribing**. If this is not going to solve the problem you may need to **refer** the patient to a specialist or to another team member.

Sometimes **hospital admission** is appropriate. I will discuss each of these steps in the next few sections.

• *Prescribing*
Before discussing what to prescribe we need to discuss the decision *whether* to prescribe. It is often stated that the first ethical principle is to *do no harm* and although it *is* possible to have done some harm by this stage in the consultation the risks start to get much higher as soon as you reach for the prescription pad. Doctors (and many patients) often overestimate the benefits of drugs and underestimate the side effects. Offering the patient a prescription immediately medicalises the problem, with implications in terms of how seriously the patient perceives the problem both now and for the future, with knock-on effects on future help-seeking behaviour.

Sometimes you can recommend an over-the-counter treatment that can be bought without a prescription. This does to some extent reduce the medicalisation and will not require you to see the patient to issue prescriptions if the problem recurs, but the issues are the same with respect to the ratio between benefit and risk.

• *Prescription pads*

In the CSA you will be provided with some dummy FP10 prescriptions which will look almost identical to the prescriptions used by an NHS GP. Do not worry too much about putting all the patient's details on there — the patient's name is enough. The drug name and dose are however important, as may be the quantity. Use the drug's generic name rather than the proprietary one unless there is a good reason to (there are certain drugs that should be prescribed by proprietary name, usually controlled release drugs or those where bioavailability varies between preparations).

Choose your drug carefully. Some registrars seem to throw evidence-based medicine out of the window when they think it is mainly consulting skills being tested, but the CSA is a test of your clinical skills and the examiners will be keen to see that you prescribe appropriately. You need to get into the habit of thinking explicitly about why you prescribe the drugs you do. Whenever you prescribe in your normal surgeries get into the habit of thinking about how you would justify each prescription to your trainer if he were to ask you to. Ask yourself the following questions:

■ What are the particular features of the drug you are prescribing?
■ Why is this drug better than the alternatives?
■ Are there any specific guidelines for the condition you are treating?
■ How many tablets should you prescribe
■ Are there any safety issues such as risk of overdose?

When you have made your choice you need to make sure you give the patient information about the drug you have prescribed, and this includes how and when it should be taken and any side effects to expect. You should also check that this has been understood and see if the patient has any questions about it.

• *Dealing with prescription requests*

It is possible that you might see a patient where issuing a prescription is the main focus of the consultation, for example where a patient is asking for a specific drug to be prescribed, or where the patient has seen a consultant or other colleague who is recommending a particular treatment.

It is likely in this case that the drug will be something you might not feel terribly comfortable prescribing. This might be because it is a drug you do not know enough about, an 'alternative' therapy, a very expensive drug, or one that is not actually licensed for the condition the patient has.

While it might seem that the challenge in these cases is how much you actually know about the drug, in reality the 'nub' of the case is likely to centre on the negotiation with the patient, how well you manage to set out the advantages and disadvantages of prescribing the drug and negotiate a mutually acceptable way forward. There is an element of honesty involved and you should be prepared to set out the reasons for your reticence clearly but sensitively to the patient. Do not forget that while you might be able to pull the wool over the patient's eyes the examiner will not be fooled by spurious rules or guidelines that prevent you prescribing it, so only refer to guidelines that really exist and make sure you recall them accurately.

Think about what negotiation actually means — it does not mean just saying no! It generally means that there is a constructive dialogue between the two parties. It is important to find out as much as you can about why the patient thinks the treatment might be helpful and try not to be dismissive. Your decision will need to be based on a balance between doing good (beneficence), not doing harm (non-maleficence), the patient's autonomy, and the broader implications for the NHS (distributive justice) in the case of a very expensive drug.

If you do decide the requested drug is not something you are prepared to prescribe (and of course sometimes it **is** right for a doctor to say no), you will then need to be able to justify this to the patient and be able to offer the patient some other way forward.

In today's society patient autonomy carries a lot of weight. This is quite rightly so, but while a patient has a right to choose a treatment that might have potential for harm, do not forget that you as a professional also have autonomy and the right to decline to be party to that treatment. If society intended patients to have total autonomy over what drugs they take we would not have a 'prescription only' category for drugs. The examiners will want you to facilitate the patient making an informed choice but a line has to be drawn somewhere.

• *Referral*

You may come across a patient in the CSA who requires a referral. This referral may be to any other health professional, for example to someone else within your primary health care team (physiotherapist, counsellor), a local consultant or even as an emergency admission.

For the purposes of the CSA you should assume you are working in a 'normal' NHS general practice with the usual array of facilities and team members and with a district general hospital available. It is probably easiest for you to imagine yourself back in your own practice, and to consider the facilities you have available there.

Do not be tempted to offer a referral as an easy way out of what you perceive to be a tricky problem, and this applies to in-house referrals as well as those to secondary care. If the problem is one that the examiners feel you should manage within the consultation or within primary care you will be penalised for failing to do that. It may well be that the patient might give you some hints about this, but beware the patient who is a 'denier' and does not want to go to hospital despite having a potentially life-threatening condition!

If you do offer a referral, the patient may well ask you how long it is likely to be before they receive an appointment. Make sure that you are realistic in any estimates you give — it might be tempting to reassure them that they will be seen in neurology outpatients in a couple of weeks for their headaches, but the examiner is likely to take a dim view of such 'white lies'. A long wait may result in the patient putting you under pressure to come up with an alternative management plan.

If it is the patient who is requesting the referral, approach the request as you would with a prescription demand as discussed previously. Do not to overlook the negative aspects of a referral — not only are there resource implications, getting onto the hospital conveyor belt can have negative implications for patients in terms of over-medicalisation, and unpleasant investigations. You should always explore whether the problem might be better dealt with in primary care or using other resources.

### 5.6.6 Involving the patient

When considering your management plan you should ensure that you involve the patient in the decision-making. This particular aspect of consulting skills was one of the more challenging parts of the MRCGP video exam, partly because it is genuinely quite challenging to do well but also because many candidates looked like they were attempting it in their video consultations without having really practised it much. As a consequence their attempts often looked a little wooden and contrived. Many seemed to take the literal wording of the exam's performance criterion which used the term 'sharing management options' without really considering why it was there and what it really meant. It is far better to think in terms of 'involving the patient' in management decisions, establishing their preferences regarding treatment and taking those into consideration appropriately.

Of course there are times when things are fairly clear cut and there is only one appropriate course of action, or where some of the management options are inappropriate for various reasons. It has already been pointed out that being patient-centred does not simply mean doing what the patient wants, so for example faced with a patient presenting with a serious or life-threatening condition whose initial approach is to deny the problem you probably need to spend some time persuading them to accept appropriate management. Similarly, you should not offer inappropriate management options, for example antibiotics for a patient with a self-limiting upper respiratory infection.

The first step in involving the patient is to define what management options are appropriate and available to you. First of all think carefully about whether you really do need to do anything or if a 'wait and see' approach is reasonable. Factors to consider include the likelihood of a bad outcome if you do not do something, the likely benefit of any treatment you might offer balanced by the potential harm of the treatment.

Establish the individual patient's personal preferences; some patients are generally averse to taking tablets and would rather tolerate symptoms than resort to medication, while others have a 'pill for every ill' mindset. Some patients are fairly fatalistic and may prefer not to be terribly interventionist while others will want to investigate every symptom and leave no stone unturned in a quest for symptom control or risk reduction. Some patients prefer the more old-fashioned treatments, while others have faith in new technology. Some patients have a pathological fear of hospitals and investigations. Preferences may well be volunteered but otherwise it is your job to discover them.

Patients' previous experiences, or those of their friends and family may have a bearing on their preferences. For example, a patient who knows a relative who has had a serious operative complication will not be reassured by the statistic that show that it happens in less than 1 in 1000 cases. The way the media present risk also influences patients — for example parents are terrified of their child dying of meningitis even though the absolute risk is low (Edwards et al, 2002; Elwyn et al, 1999). Consider the case scenarios opposite:

## 5.7 Challenging scenarios

This section will cover the *set pieces* of the CSA — those scenarios that are very likely to turn up in one guise or another. You will experience a wide variety of clinical scenarios when you sit the CSA, but there are certain to be some recurring themes. Although the scenarios may change from one sitting of an exam to another (the patient's name, age and sex, the actual condition), the issues to be dealt with in many of the consultations will recur. In this section I will present some 'generic' issues that are likely to occur and discuss how you should attempt to deal with them.

First of all though, a 'warning'. Use this section to prepare you for what to expect but do not take any of these example too literally; they are here to give you some examples and to demonstrate how some of the problems are generalisable as are the skills you use to tackle them. I will refer to the risks of trying to 'learn' cases in the section on pitfalls later on. The scenarios described below are not based on any knowledge of the actual CSA case bank, they are derived from reflection on what skills the examiners would like to test that can feasibly be tested in the CSA format. If you keep a diary of the cases you see in a typical week in general practice and grade them in terms of challenge, you will probably find lots of these appear in that list. You might identify some others yourself.

### 5.7.1 Breaking bad news

This is probably one of the more challenging scenarios. There are lots of

**Case scenario: Inguinal hernia**

**A patient presents with an inguinal hernia.**

**Doctor-centred approach**: referral to a surgeon

**Patient-centred approach**: Consider this patient's risks of developing problems if the hernia is left untreated. Assess any other ongoing medical problems that impinge on their anaesthetic risk?
*Asses other physical factors*: is the hernia actually giving the patient any trouble; are age and mobility factors?
*Consider the status of the patient*: a young fit manual worker would undoubtedly see this differently compared to an elderly diabetic. Do not make any assumptions

**Case scenario: Raised blood pressure**

**How do you treat a patient who has had a series of three blood pressure readings over the previous few months all just above the recommended treatment threshold?**

**Doctor-centred approach**: follow guidelines (e.g. NICE) and tell the patient they need treatment

**Patient-centred approach**: make a more customised risk-assessment for the patient and try to help them understand the risks and benefits. In reality unless you have a particularly high-risk patient the absolute benefit of drug treatment is fairly low with high NNTs. Some patients will want to get onto treatment as soon as possible whereas others might prefer to explore other non-medical approaches through diet and exercise etc.

possible clinical scenarios, but the main point of the case is the same: you will be imparting some bad news to the patient.

This will generally be fairly obvious and you are likely to be given a result in the form of a straight test result such as an X-ray, scan, or blood test, or possibly a letter from a consultant. The diagnosis could be a malignancy, but there are other possibilities such as neurological disorders such as multiple sclerosis or motor neurone disease. You may well be given the diagnosis in the patient notes, so you may have a couple of minutes before the patient comes in to gather your thoughts and do a little planning. There is not likely to be much preamble in the consultation as the examiners will want you to get to the main issue quickly

— ten minutes is not a long time to deal with it.

Your first thoughts might be about the actual condition itself. You must reassure yourself that you are not expected to have specialist knowledge of the condition. Of course you do need *some* factual knowledge, but by the time you sit this exam you are likely to have been a qualified doctor for at least three years and you will have had at least six months experience in general practice, so you are not likely to encounter anything that completely flummoxes you. Remind yourself that a case like this is designed to test your communication skills and your empathy.

The first principle in breaking bad news is choosing a time and place, but of course this is all outside your control in the CSA! You can make sure you are seated close to the patient without a desk intervening between you. The patient's opening statement is likely to be something such as: *'I've come for my test results doctor'*, or *'You asked me to come and see you'*.

Find out what the patient knows or suspects already. You can do this by asking the patient what their understanding of the purpose of the test was, or to ask them to recap their main symptoms and establish what they think might be wrong using the techniques we discussed earlier in this chapter.

* *Prepare the patient*
What you do next will depend on whether the patient indicates that they suspect something serious or not. If they do not seem to suspect it is something serious then it is generally recommended that you give them warning early on that you have bad news for them. There is a balance to be struck — you need to be open, honest and direct but a the same time to deliver the information sensitively and not be too direct initially. You could say something such as: *'Well I'm sorry but the test results are quite serious'*, or *'I'm afraid I have some bad news for you'*. You then need to pause to let it sink in and give the patient a chance to respond. As always you need to respond appropriately to the patient's reaction and it is no good learning set phrases for this.

If the patient still gives no indication of any specific suspicions you need to give them the news, preferably slowly, a bit at a time and using language they will understand. If the patient does seem to have suspicions you ought to establish what those suspicions are and confirm the diagnosis for them, again taking time and not giving too much information at once.

In the CSA your patient is likely to be alone, but it is worth asking at this stage if they would prefer to have someone with them, and offer to contact a partner or friend. You might also like to ask if they would prefer to defer further discussion until they can come back with someone.

* *Use of language*
When discussing the diagnosis language is of course vitally important. Giving patients serious diagnoses is an unpleasant task and is often difficult emotionally

for the doctor too. All too often this leads doctors to use slightly vague terms or ones which are a bit ambiguous, talking about 'shadows' on chest x-rays, or a 'mass' in the abdomen. The terms 'benign' and 'malignant' have very clear meaning to us as doctors but probably not to most patients. What patients want to know is whether they have cancer or not, and it is best not to avoid this issue and to actually use the word 'cancer' since it removes any ambiguity completely. You really must take time to check that the patient understands what you are telling them, and to ask them if they have any questions.

- *Patient reaction*

Patients will react in many different ways, whether it is in your own consulting room or in the CSA they can be upset and tearful, or simply go very quiet and reflective. Some may even be angry, particularly if there has been any delay in the diagnosis. You must respond appropriately with empathy. This may involve silence on your part, using touch such as placing a hand on the patient's arm or verbal expressions such as *'I'm sorry, I know this is really difficult for you'*. Simply acknowledging their reaction can be useful, for example: *'I can see that you're quite shocked/angry'*. It might be worth checking again if they would prefer you to contact someone to accompany them.

Most patients will want to know something about what treatment can be offered and their prognosis. As a GP you may well feel unable to be too specific about this, and most patients will be referred on to specialist care, but it is important that you do attempt to give them some indications as to what sort of treatment to expect. It is important to emphasise that you will be able to do something, to give the patient some hope, but without being inappropriately optimistic. Giving prognoses is fraught with problems and is generally best avoided, especially in the initial stages.

Your patient will want to know what is going to happen next and it is important that you are very specific and very clear about this. If their diagnosis is one of cancer, or potentially so, make them aware of the specific rules within the NHS for managing this, for example the 'two-week rule'. Reassure them that they will be prioritised and that you will make sure they are seen quickly.

At times like these patients need to feel supported, and like to know exactly what is going to happen and who to contact. It is a time when a GP taking personal responsibility really does help, so it is important that you stress your availability to the patient, and let them know how they can contact you. It might be helpful to arrange a specific time for them to come back so you can clarify any questions they might have, to see them with a partner or close relative if they would like that, and to let them know how you are progressing with their referral.

If the patient is distraught think about asking if they would like a quiet room to sit in to recover, and ask if someone can come to collect them if they came alone.

A consultation where you are breaking bad news is likely to be emotionally draining (you may be shocked at how well the role-players can play such roles!). During your normal surgeries you can take a bit of time out after a difficult consultation (deal with a couple of phone calls or grab a cup of coffee), but you cannot do this in the CSA and your next patient is only a couple of minutes away. Move on mentally and emotionally as soon as the patient has left the room. Do not sit there dwelling on how well or badly you think you handled the consultation. Get on with reading the notes for your next patient and start to gather your thoughts about how you are going to tackle the next consultation.

### 5.7.2 Consultations with children

You may have a consultation with a child in the CSA, and if so it is likely they will be accompanied by a parent or guardian. Do not lose sight of who your patient is — in reality it is both of them although the child is of course the prime consideration.

Although the parent is likely to do a lot of the talking you really must do your best to engage with the child at an appropriate level. That means putting them at their ease by being relaxed and friendly, facing the child and maintaining eye contact with them while asking questions rather than looking at the parent. If the parent answers your questions anyway (as they often tend to do), you can still try to involve the child by seeking confirmation or further clarification of the parent's answers. Obviously much of this will depend on the age and maturity of the child, but in reality presenting you with very young children in the CSA is unlikely as the child will have to be old enough to understand the role and the sort of responses they will be expected to provide.

* *Confidentiality and consent*
If you think the child is mature enough you may feel it useful to have a chat to them alone. This can be tricky to tell the parents, but if phrased appropriately most parents will understand. You need to ask also if the child is happy to have a chat alone. It might be important to explain to an older child the issues around confidentiality, as most will be unaware that you have a duty to respect their confidentiality. It can facilitate the conversation if you reassure them that before the parent comes back into the room the two of you will agree what is divulged. Whatever their maturity remember that a child is unlikely to divulge information regarding drug or alcohol use, sexual activity and contraception with a parent present.

The legalities around consent and confidentiality are complex and not always intuitive. With older children the issue of competence arises — you may have heard of the phrases 'Gillick competence' and 'Fraser competence', referring to the names involved in the famous legal case that set precedent. Is this child mature enough to be able to make their own decisions and take responsibility for themselves? There is no quick and easy way of doing this, in reality much of our assessments are subconscious as we take in the patient's general demeanour and use of language, but you must make sure you explicitly check their understanding of the issues raised in the consultation.

You can get information from the parent too; they will probably have an opinion about whether the child is able to decide things for themselves. Your problem arises when you think the child is competent but the parent wants to make the decisions!

When it comes to negotiating management plans the ideal situation is to keep both parent and child happy, but again the child is the more important of the two. You really must involve both in the discussion.

### 5.7.3 Cultural issues

Language may be one obvious barrier — engaging in the subtleties of the consulting skills we have discussed is a whole new ball game if it has to be done via an interpreter (whether the interpreter is present in the room or whether they are on the end of the phone as in when you use Language Line).

Some cultures may be much more deferential to a doctor and might expect a much more doctor-centred approach than you have been encouraged to utilise. Even non-verbal communication can be confusing — avoiding eye contact may indicate respect rather than embarrassment, for example.

Different cultures will have different attitudes towards medicine, with many being far more likely to expect a more medicalising approach than we are used to in the UK.

Muslim women may not wish to be uncovered for a clinical examination, so it is even more important to sensitively ask permission to examine and be prepared to compromise; a slightly inadequate examination through clothes may well be better than no examination at all, but be prepared to be a little more persuasive if there is a potentially serious problem.

### 5.7.4 An angry patient

Dealing with anger is a challenging skill, and in the context of a consultation even more so since the patient's anger will often arise from a potential shortcoming on our own part or of a colleague.

Patients get angry for all sorts of reasons, sometimes because they think we have made an error or not helped them as much as they would have liked, but sometimes because they think a colleague of ours has let them down. Sometimes it can just be from frustration that medicine in general is unable to help them, or because of shortcomings of the system within the NHS (for example a long waiting list or a rationed treatment).

Of course the principles of managing an angry patient or even one who is just unhappy are similar no matter what the cause. We often need to curtail our natural reactions which are generally to be angry back or to run and take cover!

The first thing is to try to remain calm yourself and concentrate on the skills you are going to use to manage the situation. Your active listening skills are important in these cases, so make it obvious to the patient that you are listening and that you are interested in hearing what they have to say.

Acknowledging their feelings is important. Try saying something such as: '*I can see you're pretty angry about this...*', or '*This has clearly upset you*'.

Use the skills we have discussed earlier to establish exactly what the patient is angry about and what their expectations of you are. You need to establish all the facts so you have got a clear idea what has happened, summarising it back to the patient can ensure you have understood correctly. You can do all this without actually expressing any opinion, you should try to remain neutral — we naturally find this difficult if the patient is blaming us for something or if they are blaming a colleague, as doctors we generally have a natural loyalty to our partners, staff, even the local systems in which we work.

You do not need to admit fault on anyone's behalf at this stage; a statement such as: '*I can see why that would upset you*' expresses understanding and empathy for their emotion without accepting any blame.

Once you have completed your information gathering you can start to analyse the situation. Sometimes you might think the patient is being completely unreasonable, and at others you might well agree that they have been hard done by, but you should attempt to remain neutral. No matter what the patient tells you it is more than likely that you will need to get information from elsewhere to corroborate or triangulate, and you should sensitively explain this to them. If the patient is made to feel that you are taking their concerns seriously and that you will look into the situation it is likely they will be calmer and be happy to work with you constructively to solve the problem.

- *Making a complaint*

What you should not do is either behave very defensively or collude with them in criticising a colleague. Being defensive will make them feel you are not going to help them, and criticising a colleague is potentially unprofessional. If you think a colleague (or even you yourself) has behaved or acted inappropriately, it might be acceptable to say that it does look like that may be possible, but that you will need to establish more information and hear the colleague's side of the story first. If the patient is unhappy about a colleague within the practice it might be appropriate to offer to arrange to meet them with the patient. If there is potential for a complaint you should facilitate this and explain how to go about this constructively.

Of course sometimes patients really are downright unreasonable and if so you will need to address this at some stage; if the patient has unrealistic expectations of what a doctor or staff member can do, of what medicine in general can do or of what the NHS can reasonably provide, then you might need to attempt to sensitively manage those expectations.

There might be scope for you to do something to put the situation right, for example in arranging or expediting a hospital appointment, or in providing appropriate treatment yourself. You should say that you will do what you can to put the situation right to the patient's satisfaction, but beware making it seem that you are doing this to distract from dealing with the cause of the patient's emotion.

Make sure the consultation ends with an agreed plan of action with a definite timescale. Let the patient know you will be happy to speak to them again — taking personal responsibility and providing continuity is important.

### 5.7.5 A disabled patient

Patients present with all sorts of disability, but clearly within the context of the CSA there is a limit on what you might meet. It might be as simple as a patient with a walking stick or crutches, but you may encounter a blind or deaf patient.

Acknowledge the disability rather than pretend it is not there, and think of ways you can help the patient. Try to imagine being that patient and what effect the disability might have on coming to see a doctor. The patient might need to be guided to a chair for example, or you might need to move your chair to accommodate a wheelchair. You are unlikely to meet a profoundly deaf patient in the CSA as it would probably make the consultation just too challenging, but you might have a patient who is partially deaf where you need to speak loudly and clearly.

Make sure you continue to take the disability into consideration throughout the consultation, and ask yourself if the patient needs any help from you (for example in undressing or getting dressed again). Consider the disability in formulating and negotiating your management plan — do not make assumptions about what the patient can or cannot do, and ask them if they think they will be able to manage. Disabled patients do not like being patronised, and those with long-term disabilities are often more capable than we would imagine.

### 5.7.6 Hidden agendas

A hidden agenda is when a patient presents with a problem but the actual main problem is not the presenting complaint. Sometimes the presenting complaint can be a complete red herring, in which case it is sometimes referred to as a token presentation.

Patients do this for a couple of reasons. Often because they are worried you will think they are neurotic, or because they are embarrassed or ashamed about the problem they have, or sometimes because they are in a form of denial. In this case they might 'check you out' with something fairly innocuous, and if they find you sympathetic and consider they can trust you they may then divulge the real problem that is on their mind. At other times the presenting complaint is the main problem but there is some hidden fear or anxiety that you have to work at uncovering.

How do you know if there might be a hidden agenda? It can be very difficult, but the key thing is to gain the patient's trust by being empathic and a good listener. Sometimes there will be cues or hints that there is something else on their mind, for example pauses, failure to maintain eye contact or generally looking uncomfortable.

In the CSA the patient is likely to give you more of a chance than in 'real life', and they will be consciously giving you cues. However the actors are very well trained and highly skilled and if you do not establish good rapport and you do not make them feel they trust you they will withhold cues.

If you suspect there is something else on the patient's mind you should probe carefully, acknowledging the signs you have identified, for example by saying '*You're looking worried*', or '*You seem as if there's something else on your mind*'. Be prepared to use silence, and if you still think there is something else you can ask directly if there is anything they are worried about. Sometimes you might be able to second guess what it is as we discussed previously. When you think you know what is going on it is useful again to summarise it back to check that you are grasping the issues correctly.

### 5.7.7 Psychosocial problems

A high proportion of the patients we see in general practice are presenting with problems that have a psychosocial basis and this will be reflected in the CSA.

You could be presented with a patient with depression, anxiety, phobia, obsessive compulsive disorder or any other psychiatric conditions. Patients sometimes present to us with distress resulting from their social circumstances, and it is important that you are able to explore these appropriately and differentiate between what is a social problem and what is an illness. For example not all patients who are unhappy are actually depressed. There are two issues in these consultations:

- Identifying psychological illness
- Putting patients problems into a psychosocial context

Diagnosing psychological illness is like diagnosing any other illness; you take a history, encouraging the patient to tell you their story, and find out what they think about the problem (as we have discussed already). Then you must conduct an examination, in this case not a physical one but a psychological one. It is important that you ask all the right questions to explore their illness fully — by the time you get this far you should have a good idea of what the problem is and therefore tailor your questions appropriately.

- *Assess severity*
You need to establish the severity of the illness; if you have a depressed patient it

is really important that you establish the degree of risk of self-harm. This should have been done to death in your teaching sessions with your trainer, but do not forget it in the exam! There are various ways of doing this, from asking directly if they have actually considered suicide (which can sometimes be appropriate) to the more subtle: *'Have you ever felt so low that you've considered hurting yourself?'*. We all see patients who say they are suicidal but actually are not, so if they do express suicidal thoughts you need to check this out by perhaps asking things such as how they thought they might do it or what has stopped them from doing it. Similarly if you have a patient who says they are hearing voices you need to find out how often it happens, what sort of things the voices say and how distressing they find it. If you think you have a psychotic patient you then must explore whether they represent a risk to others.

- *Social context*

The other issue is to put the patient's problems into a social context. Whether the problem is physical or psychological you must explore the social aspects, and there is so much more to this than merely asking what they do for a living, whether they are married or how many children they have. By all means ask what their job is, but even more importantly, how does their illness affect their ability to do it? Is the illness affecting their relationships at home, what does the patient's wife/husband/partner think about the problem? Does it affect their hobbies?

Consider how medical conditions might affect your own lifestyle — what if it prevented you from driving, playing golf, tennis, etc? How would you feel about that?

### 5.7.8 third parties

You will probably recognise that we often have a third party involved in a consultation, either because they come with the patient but sometimes because they come on a patient's behalf.

For example, consider a patient attending with a friend or relative. You need to consider why the third party is there. The obvious answer is that they are there at the patient's request to give some moral support, but do not make assumptions! Very often the patient might say: *"I hope you don't mind my partner coming in with me?"*, in which case at least you know who the other person is and the implication then is that they are there with the patient's consent.

On the other hand the other person might say something such as: *"I'm John's wife, do you mind if I come in with him?"*, in which case you might be left wondering whose idea it was that she attend with him, or indeed whose idea it was that he come to the doctor in the first place!

In each of these scenarios you are given the opportunity to check that your patient is happy to be accompanied — for the latter you might say something like

'*You're very welcome so long as John doesn't mind*'. If there is no introduction it is reasonable to ask who the other person is, and to ask the patient if they would rather consult you with them present or if they would rather see you alone.

Remember that while the other person might be there with good intentions, and while you do not want to offend them, your first duty is to the patient, and you must always bear in mind that it may be that they would rather see you on their own, at least for some of the consultation.

Even if the third party is there at the patient's request the consultation may stray into personal or sensitive areas that might lead you to suspect that their continued presence could be inhibitory, in which case it is your job to suggest that perhaps it would be helpful to have a chat with the patient alone. Sometimes patients are genuinely nervous about coming to the doctor and do appreciate the support of a friend or relative accompanying them, but once they are there it is likely that your communication skills will put them at ease so that they no longer need them there.

Sometimes the third party will speak for the patient, in which case it is generally best to thank them for trying to help but to gently say that you find it more useful to hear it in the patient's own words. They may even try to take charge of the consultation, which makes it a little more difficult. In this case try to see if you can get by with a little diplomacy and prompting the patient, but if it is becoming disruptive it is best to take charge and ask if you could have a moment with the patient alone.

- *A third party presenting without the patient*

Next we need to consider the third party presenting without the patient. If this is a parent presenting on behalf of a child then it makes life easier in that confidentiality is less of an issue, especially for younger children.

In the case of a presumably competent adult it is more difficult. It is important to let the person know that you do appreciate their concern but to gently remind them that you cannot really have much of a two way conversation since you cannot discuss the patient's medical issues without consent. A common scenario is a son or daughter expressing concern about an elderly parent. You need to remember the rules of confidentiality which are that you cannot breach it unless (in this scenario) you have the patient's explicit consent or you are fully confident that the breach is in the patient's best interests. It is fine to gather information from the relative but with the understanding that it is a one way conversation. Sometimes relatives make it more difficult for you by asking you not to disclose the conversation to the patient, and although this can sometimes be justified, you must proceed with caution.

Lay people generally underestimate the confidentiality issues and often fail to see the pitfalls in a deception, but it is often very difficult to avoid the deception being uncovered — which can have disastrous consequences for the doctor/patient relationship.

Another common scenario you may recognise is that of a relative not wanting a patient to be told the full extend of the truth about a terminal diagnosis, which does of course beg the question how they knew about it before the patient in the first place! In this case it is almost never appropriate to collude with the request, you must discuss the situation with the patient themselves and come to your own conclusion about how much it is appropriate to tell them. Of course you will need to explain carefully to the relative the rules under which you must operate as a doctor and explain why it is a bad idea to lie to your patient.

- *Health professionals consulting*

A similar but slightly different scenario is when another health professional consults about a patient. This is quite different in that if this is someone who is involved in providing care for the patient you do have the right to discuss confidential medical information with them.

In this context what you must do is consider the different roles the two of you have in providing care for the patient and how you can work synergistically to maximise team-working and enhance the care provided. Try to consider the specific skills each of you brings to the partnership, clarify exactly why the other professional has approached you and find out, and what they thought you might do. Consider the information they bring to you and ask yourself what else you need to know before contemplating any action. Perhaps you need to arrange to assess the patient first. Make sure you do not get coerced into something you might later regret!

### 5.7.9 'Expert' patients

In this section we will consider the issues raised by a patient who has an in-depth knowledge of the medical problem they have, either because they, are just generally well-informed and have researched it for themselves, or perhaps they themselves have a medical qualification.

Doctors may often find this sort of scenario quite threatening — we are worried they might know more than us and expose inadequate knowledge on our part, or perhaps the patients come with very specific ideas and expectations that might not match what we consider to be appropriate.

Another issue is that we must not make assumptions — it is easy to be seduced by a patient who uses lots of medical jargon into believing they are better informed than they actually are. You must remember that the person in front of you is still your patient and that you are the person with the responsibility for making sure the decisions taken are medically appropriate and that your patient fully understands whatever is going on and is taking well informed decisions.

On the other hand do not be patronising — it can be a delicate balancing act, and as with any other patient you must explore their understanding and expectations explicitly but you should make sure that you acknowledge and value their expertise.

• *Equality*

You must also bear in mind equality. Equality in this context doe not mean treating everyone exactly the same; it means treating people according to their circumstances and their needs but being mindful of the needs of others — the issue of distributive justice.

A doctor who consults you about a medical problem will actually have quite different needs to your average lay person — doctors tend to be infrequent consulters and usually self-manage and self-treat minor problems, sometimes major ones too, and often deny there is anything wrong until quite late on in the course of an illness. By the time a doctor present with a set of symptoms they are far more likely to have significant pathology than other patients, and therefore it might be quite appropriate to make yourself a little more accessible and to take their concerns a little more seriously. This is not favouritism; it is acknowledging and responding to different needs.

However beware of the colleague or well informed patient who expects you to ignore usual practice or protocols, prescribe inappropriate treatments or refer when it is not necessary. You must always negotiate a management plan that you are comfortable with.

## 5.8 Safety

As the *n*MRCGP is a licensing exam for general practice there is a lot of emphasis on safety. Make sure that in your quest for demonstrating your communication skills and patient-centred approach you do not overlook the clinical medicine. In addition to all the active listening and exploring patient agendas you must also take a systematic medical history, conduct a competent clinical examination where appropriate and that your management plan is in keeping with current accepted evidence-based practice.

## 5.9 Resource issues

We have already touched on the subject of resource usage and this section is a quick reminder that the CSA is about general practice in the UK, and that your consultations should take account of some of the vagaries of working within the NHS. One of the principal restrictions on the way GPs practise is that we work within a system that has limited resources. Some treatments are explicitly rationed, for example treatments for impotence or infertility, while others are much more subtle such as the way waiting lists operate and the guidance we receive on prescribing generally.

It is tempting in consultations to try to keep the patient happy, and you will feel under this pressure within the CSA. Being a GP in the UK however is about balancing the wants and needs of the individual patient in front of us with the broader needs of our practice population.

In some clinical areas there is specific guidance from NICE and you will no doubt have revised many of their treatment guidelines in preparing for the AKT. It is important that you do not mentally discard that information when you sit the CSA, since presenting you with a case that involves negotiating with a patient about a treatment where there is a rationing issue offers the examiners an opportunity to present you with multiple challenges.

## 5.10 The Quality and Outcomes Framework

GPs in the UK were presented with a new contract in 2004 which included the 'Quality and Outcomes Framework' generally referred to as QOF. This incentivised GPs to pursue targets in key areas of practice, mainly in the realms of chronic disease management. This has impinged on the day-to-day consultations of GPs as they opportunistically gather the data required to meet the targets and thus boost their income. There are many concerns about the effect of this on everyday practice, not least the way in which it can disrupt the consultation. Most of the guidance in this chapter on consulting with patients has been encouraging you to be patient-centred and to focus on the patient's agenda. The QOF targets tend to push GPs in the opposite agenda by encouraging us to address issues other than the ones the patient has presented about, and to practice in a much more disease-centred way.

There is good news for you — you can more or less forget about the QOF during the CSA. First of all you will not have a computer system to worry about, so there will be no pop-up prompts to check the patient's blood pressure, etc. Second, the examiners recognise that you have got your hands full dealing with what are generally fairly challenging consultations in the ten minutes allowed, so they really do not expect you to attempt any opportunistic health promotion. For the purpose of the CSA, do not ask about smoking status, blood pressures, whether the patient has had a smear, etc. unless it is directly relevant to the presenting problem.

## 5.11 How the cases are marked

The first thing to say in this section is that you should not worry too much about how the questions are marked! This section is here just to help you understand the process, and hopefully to reassure you.

* *Assesors*

Each patient you see in the CSA will be accompanied by an assessor. The assessors are all experienced GPs and all have gone through a rigorous selection process followed by specific training for the CSA. In addition to this there is rigorous quality assurance to monitor their performance. Most have been examiners for the 'old' MRCGP, but there are many new recruits, most of whom are experienced GP trainers.

Each assessor will be accompanying a patient for the whole day and will therefore only be marking the one case. This means that the assessors can very reliably 'calibrate' for the case they are watching; they have very in-depth knowledge of the case and will have been involved in a calibration exercise for that case along with their role-player and the other role-players and examiners who are involved in that case for the day. They will have a good idea of all the various permutations of approaches candidates could possibly take with the case and have a very clear idea of the level of performance required to achieve a pass for that case.

- *Three domains*

The assessor will make an overall global decision on your performance in the case deciding whether you have clearly passed or failed it or have been a borderline pass or fail. Although it is a global decision, the marking schedule is subdivided into three domains, and for each of these the assessor will award a clear or borderline pass or fail. The assessor will use these three grades to guide the overall decision, but they are not used in a simplistic mathematical way, so you could still pass the case even if you perform badly in one of the domains, and similarly you could still fail even if you did reasonably well in two of the domains. This may sound a bit vague and unscientific, but a guiding principle in the assessment's development has been to avoid marking by check-list. The reason for this is because marking complex behavioural skills and the problem solving and integrative skills the module is designed to test is simply not possible by check-list. One of the criticisms of the 'old' video assessment was that it did seem to result in candidates resorting to using these sort of techniques which produced unnatural, dysfunctional consultations. The new assessment wants to avoid this and reward the kind of behaviours patients would regard as good doctoring — good communication and clinical skills integrated into natural, flowing consultations. The three domains are:

- Data-gathering, technical and assessment skills
- Clinical management skills
- Interpersonal skills

The reason these are distilled down from the six areas listed above is largely down to practicality — to expect an assessor to bear six different areas in mind and grade each individually is expecting a bit too much.

When you start to look at individual consultations you will realise that very few require skills from each of these three domains in equal measure, most will be heavily weighted towards one, although some will of course be fairly relatively equally balanced. That is another reason why a global assessment is an advantage over a check-list system where points are awarded for key elements of the consultation — that would require a complex weighting system whereas experienced assessors can incorporate this sort of weighting into a judgement quite easily and naturally, particularly given a little help from the case writers in spelling out the 'nub' of the case and what it's designed to test.

Global judgements are generally in your favour since they allow the assessor to balance mistakes you make against your overall performance and allow them to factor in any parts of the consultation they thought were particularly good. Examiners generally do not like failing candidates who perform well overall but make a couple of non-critical slips. Similarly they do not like passing candidates whose performance they think is generally poor but who slip in a few key words or phrases that might tick a few boxes on a marking schedule.

The three domains are pretty much self-explanatory, but we will spend a little time expanding on them to make sure you understand them.

### 5.11.1 Data-gathering, technical and assessment skills

Taking an adequate history, conducting an appropriate examination and interpreting the information gathered appropriately. This needs to be done in a systematic way with appropriate identification of key findings, it should also be done efficiently, being selective and making good use of time.

### 5.11.2 Clinical management skills

This domain refers to your decision-making skills — choosing investigations, formulating a differential diagnosis and coming up with a sensible management plan with appropriate prescribing and referral and care management. Also included is practising safely and holistically, being able to manage complex or multiple problems and encouraging a positive attitude and health promotion.

### 5.11.3 Interpersonal skills

Here the examiners are looking for your ability to connect with the patient, identifying and exploring their ideas, concerns and expectations. You also need to explain effectively and take your patients views into consideration. Also in here is the 'human' aspect of being a doctor — being understanding, considerate and sympathetic, demonstrating empathy and being non-judgemental.

On the marking schedule the assessor is provided with a series of phrases that illustrate the positive and negative features within each domain — it must be emphasised that these are not used as a check-list but to illustrate the sort of behaviour being looked for and to remind the examiner of some of the poorer examples of consulting that might appear within the domain.

At the end of the consultation the assessor will have awarded three separate domain grades and will have to decide on a single overall grade. Also on the schedule is space to record feedback — this is not in free text format but instead as a series of statements that represent a range of behaviours from which the assessor makes a selection. These can be fed back to you after the exam.

There are no 'tricks' you can use to fool the assessors. They will assess whatever they see, but will also take note of what does not go on in the consultation. Do not think that by avoiding difficult issues you will avoid potentially making mistakes and therefore losing marks — you will lose marks by avoiding issues, whether that means you just left them out completely or tried to skirt around them by arranging to refer the patient or arranging a follow-up appointment next week so you can look something up or ask a colleague about in the meantime.

The role-player takes no part in the grading, although the assessor may well confer with them before deciding your grade. They will not ask the role-player what grade they think you should have, but might clarify matters of fact with them to confirm things you said or did not say, or to check on their feelings during the consultation. While an assessor gets a very good idea whether they feel you have adequately addressed the patient's concerns or empathised appropriately they sometimes like to double-check this with the role-player.

The assessor may take a prescription into consideration, but again it is used in a global context to inform the grade rather than contributing a specific mark. As was stated earlier they are not worried about the minor technicalities of checking the patient's name and address are completed correctly, but they will be looking to see that it is an appropriate drug used in the correct dose and that you have given a sensible quantity.

As has already pointed out, a candidate who is performing well generally but makes a couple of slips is likely to pass a case. You are not expected to be perfect, and even the most expert GP would struggle to perform well against all three domains in a complex case with only ten minutes in which to do it. However there are times when mistakes are considered too critical. Generally speaking a single mistake is only likely to drag you down into the failing zone if it is a fairly significant one — one which might result in putting a patient at risk for example. This would then be reflected in your grade for the one case only.

Since the assessors are all doctors they are subject to the General Medical Council's '*Duties of a doctor*' to report a colleague whose clinical performance is at such a low standard as to put patients at risk. This does not generally mean making a single mistake, but would need to be a more systematic pattern of behaviour that caused the assessors significant concern and led them to believe that the doctor was likely to be putting patients at risk in his everyday practice. This is generally only when they have seen very chaotic behaviour, for example not listening to patients, being rude or handling the patient roughly, irrational management, etc.

So, what do you need to do to pass overall? It is all very well deciding that you have passed or failed each of the individual 12 cases, but an overall decision as to whether you have passed or failed the CSA has to be reached. This requires a process known as 'standard setting' which is very complex. Clearly expecting you to pass every case would result in an unacceptably high failure rate, but at the time of writing the number of cases you need to pass to gain a pass overall has not been decided, and may indeed not be made public when it is decided. There are many permutations of possibilities, for example passing nine out of twelve of the cases, or up to two clear fails and two borderline fails. It is impossible to come up with a formula from any kind of absolute scientific methods, so the final answer is likely to be politically influenced in terms of an acceptable percentage of candidates who fail overall.

## 5.12 Pitfalls and common mistakes

In this section we will point out some of the common errors doctors make during consultations and focus on those that will pull your grade down.

The first of these is being doctor-centred early on in the consultation: interrupting the patient, asking closed questions and missing or ignoring cues. Apart from the fact that this sort of behaviour in itself will attract a lower grade, it reduces the information you get. It will almost always result in the information you get from the patient being inferior in both quantity and quality. The role-players are trained to respond well to a patient-centred doctor who is a good listener and will give you fuller descriptions of symptoms, be more prepared to divulge their concerns and health beliefs and will generally make your life easier.

• *Examination technique*
Many registrars just think of this exam as being one about communication skills and ignore the practical clinical examination skills in both their preparation and during the exam itself. Examiners are generally concerned that there seems to be a decline in clinical skills, possibly related partly to the reduced amount of time young doctors spend with patients these days due to shorter working hours in the junior hospital posts, but also probably to an increased reliance on technology (blood tests, X-rays, ultrasound scans, MRIs and CTs).

Examiners have observed that in the examination many registrars seem to appear to go through the motions of conducting an examination but without appearing to be actively seeking physical signs. For example, it is no good simply placing your stethoscope on the patient's chest in what appear to be the correct places, you need to be actively thinking about what you should be hearing there and about what abnormalities you might expect to find.

A third issue is that already referred to earlier in this chapter of avoiding issues. Do not try to fob the patient off — make sure you really do try to address their concerns. Think carefully before suggesting arranging investigations or a referral: is this a problem you can make progress with by good clinical decision-making? The role-players know what is the most appropriate management for their clinical problem and will probably give you cues if you are following a course that will not reward you well on the marking schedule! If you suggest seeing them again after tests or making a referral and the patient seems a little dissatisfied with this, just think again and double check whether your course of action is really the most appropriate.

Lots of candidates seem to resort to handing the patient an imaginary information leaflet. Whilst this can be a useful strategy it should not be used as an alternative to a good explanation. It is sometimes a tempting strategy to use if you are not entirely sure of the facts about the condition you are dealing with, or if you are not confident of them and are worried about explaining the problem in front of the examiner and getting bits of it wrong. In which case be honest and explain to the patient that you cannot recall all the facts but tell them what you can before resorting to the leaflet. Another reason for using them is to save time — it is much quicker to hand over a leaflet than to spend three or four minutes explaining something to a patient and answering their questions. This again is not generally a good reason, it tends to leave patients feeling like they have been fobbed off; patients would usually rather a doctor explain something than read a leaflet. In any case patients can usually access the information you are giving in the leaflet for themselves via the internet these days.

- *Making the diagnosis explicit*

Candidates sometimes initiate a treatment without actually making the diagnosis or the actual reason for the treatment explicit to the patient. If you have not explained it clearly to the patient the examiner might be left wondering too! Do not just imply diagnoses, spell them out clearly. It is particularly important when prescribing when you have reached some particular threshold.

Examples might include prescribing antibiotics for a respiratory infection, initiating an antihypertensive treatment, or giving an asthmatic a course of steroids. You need to make it explicit to the patient exactly why you are prescribing rather than adopting an expectant approach.

- *Serious diagnoses*

Another problem area is that of the more serious diagnosis that requires a specific action be taken. Candidates seem to assume that you would not be required to actually admit a patient as an emergency or section them in the exam situation — you should make no assumptions but simply concentrate on making good clinical decisions and taking the appropriate action.

### 5.12.1 Learning cases

You may find examples of CSA cases that have been 'leaked' in some way, either via an internet forum or from a course. While these can be useful in illustrating the kind of case you will need to deal with, please do be careful. The examiners and administrators are well aware of cases that have reached the public domain and make great efforts to reduce the impact of these leaks. The first step they can take is to withdraw the case completely, in which case learning it is not any use to you at all. The other thing they can do is to change the scenario so it is not immediately recognisable, or actually leave it very similar but change the emphasis or the 'nub' of the case.

Experience in the simulated surgery has shown that candidates who think they know a case tend to do badly! Firstly they make assumption based on what they have read and these assumptions can be quite misguided especially if the case has been changed. Secondly they often appear to incorporate information they have not visibly gathered, which rather gives the game away to the watching assessor! In this case the assessor will mark accordingly — you are there to demonstrate your technique, not just to come up with the correct diagnosis and treatment. Think of the cases like a maths exam where most of the marks are awarded for the methodology of how you worked the answer out rather than the actual answer itself.

## 5.13 How to prepare for the exam

We have covered lots of this as we have gone through the various aspects of the consultation, but we will recap in this section.

You have probably picked up by now that passing the CSA is about being a good doctor, and in particular being a good consulter. Hopefully you will agree that all the skills we have discussed so far in this chapter are practical, useful skills that make you an effective GP. Also that although there are things you can do on the day to improve your chances of passing, in general 'examination technique' will count for very little. So what you must do is practice being a good doctor.

• *Make use of your trainer*
Of course there is a bit more to it than simply lots of practice. You need to break down 'being a good doctor' into the specific skills to some extent to focus on each one individually to increase your ability and confidence. You must also practice integrating these individual skills into your consultations. In chapter 4 we outlined all the various parts of workplace based assessment (the multi-source feedback, patient satisfaction questionnaire, consultation observation tool, case based discussion and direct observation of procedural skills). If you thought of these as merely hurdles to get past then you have missed the point — they are there primarily to give you feedback on your performance. Although they are included in your assessment these are primarily formative assessment tools intended to help you understand your strengths and weaknesses and what

you need to do to improve.

Simply completing the tasks you need to in the WPBA will not get you very far, what you need to do is reflect on each component and consider carefully how to get the most out of it. You can do much of this unassisted, but since the vast majority of it has to be carried out while you are in your time as a GP registrar you have an additional valuable resource — your trainer. You really must make sure you get the most you can out of your trainer.

Trainers are experienced GPs with specific training in giving you the specific, individually tailored feedback you need. The nMRCGP might be a new exam but the skills required to pass it are not, and so far as consulting skills are concerned the criteria in the consultation observation tool are very similar to the performance criteria that have been used for some time in the MRCGP video component, so your trainer will be well up to speed on them.

As a GP registrar you have ample opportunity to learn — you get plenty of protected time for learning and specific teaching which for most of you will be one to one for much of it. Make sure you put this time to good use. Start video recording yourself early on in your practice attachment and use the recordings as a tool to help you improve. What you will probably find when you watch recordings of yourself consulting is that there are some areas of the consultation you naturally do better in and some you naturally find more difficult. Each week pick an individual area to work on and remind yourself of this at the start of each surgery. When you are focusing on a specific skill it is easy enough to reflect at the end of each consultation on how well it went; you do not need to have the video recorder on all the time although when you think you are getting the hang of something it is worth going over some recordings with your trainer to verify that you have indeed improved.

Generally the only time GP Registrars get to observe a skilled experienced GP consult is in their induction period at the start of their training in general practice. At that stage you are very new to the game and are often concentrating on the bigger picture of the clinical problem and are often relatively oblivious to the subtleties of the consulting skills. You might find it useful to sit in with your trainer and some of the other partners in the practice later on in your time there when you are better able to appreciate what' is going on.

Remember that patient-centred consulting is at the heart of the CSA. Registrars generally find the listening and explaining skills relatively easier to pick up and put into practice than those required to truly involve the patient in decision-making and in the management plan so you really need to focus on this. What you should find is that as you get better as it the consultations actually get easier — this should apply to all the consulting skills you are learning but particularly when it comes to formulating a management plan. That is because things are rarely black and white in general practice and there are almost always several different ways you could proceed. Getting the patient to help you with that process can actually lift the burden and make your life easier.

• *Consultation models*

We have also referred to consultation models — make sure you understand these and the different features, strengths and weaknesses of each. GP registrars generally think of them as something theoretical that they need to know about because they might get asked about it in an exam. Whilst you certainly might get asked about them in the AKT, they were developed to help us understand the complex processes going on in the doctor patient interaction so that we can understand the principles and generalise the learning to apply it elsewhere. Consider which one can help you with each different sort of problem.

• *Example cases*

The College provides some specimen cases on their website. Download these and reflect on the issues raised by each one, how you would attempt to tackle it and what you think the examiners might be looking for. You might be able to persuade your course organiser or programme director to arrange a study day with some role-players and mock cases. If not you can try it within your group without the role-players but doctors do not generally make good role-players so it is far better if you can get some local actors or role-players.

### 5.13.1 Specific examination techniques

Much of this chapter has, quite rightly, focused on communication skills, but we have also been reminded that your examination technique is important. Make sure you revisit the main bodily systems and remind yourself of a systematic approach to examining the cardiovascular system, respiratory system, the abdomen and the commonly examined parts of the neurological system.

Musculoskeletal complaints are quite easy to reproduce in CSA cases, so think of all the various complaints you might meet and remind yourself of the correct technique for examining the back, the shoulder, the hip and knee, etc. Remind yourself of any specific examination techniques that are used, look them up and make them the subject of a tutorial with your Trainer. Make sure that as well as learning how to carry out each test you discuss with your trainer the practical merits of each in actually making a diagnosis. Consider even if it would be arranging a session in the local orthopaedic clinic to observe some of these being done by the experts?

Here's a quick list of orthopaedic type problems and some of the techniques associated with them:

■ Shoulder — can you demonstrate a painful arc correctly and how to test each plane of movement?

■ Elbow — think about tennis elbow and golfer's elbow and how you diagnose each

■ Wrist — consider carpal tunnel syndrome and tenosynovitis

■ Hip — make sure you know how to demonstrate a fixed flexion deformity

■ Knee — one of the most complex joints to examine. Can you demonstrate or exclude a joint effusion, test for laxity of the collateral and cruciate ligaments, are you aware of the specific tests?

All the above are easy enough to revise and become proficient in their performance, that way you can do them fluently in the CSA.

### 5.13.2 Time management

In the MRCGP video you were allowed up to 15 minutes per consultation. This caused examiners some consternation as it did not truly reflect real life since most of us have considerably less time with patients. Also, it led to some very inefficient consulting which was frustrating to watch.

In the CSA you will only have ten minutes with each patient and your preparation must reflect this. When you start your general practice attachment you will of course need longer, but it is important that as you become more proficient you start to work on becoming more efficient and reduce your appointment times. You really should get down to ten minute appointments at least a month before sitting the CSA. Your trainer and the other partners will be well used to quicker consulting, so it might be worth sitting in a few surgeries with them to see how they keep their consulting times down and make effective use of time.

There are several key skills to time-management within a consultation. One is generally recognising when you have gathered enough information from the patient and shifting the consultation mode slightly into a rather more doctor-centred style. Another is identifying the focus of a consultation quickly and not wasting time down blind alleys. You must also become more proficient at closing consultations.

### 5.13.3 Courses

Although I will not recommend any specific courses, many registrars will go on a preparatory course for the exam. If you do decide to go on a course, research the courses, and see if you can find any feedback from previous candidates. Find out the credentials of the people running the course and doing the teaching — you do not have to be an actual examiner to teach well but of course examiners will have a greater knowledge of the exam and of what you will need to do to pass.

The College hopes to develop a scheme to 'accredit' courses which may help, but remember that just because a course is not accredited it does not mean it is no good. The converse may also be true. You should really look for courses that provide you with an opportunity to practice consultations with role-players, preferably with some expert feedback and guidance.

Make sure that if you do attend a course you do it early enough to be able to practice anything you learn — you cannot see a complex skill demonstrated one day and perform it yourself the next, it takes time and feedback.

## 5.14 Attitude

A positive mental attitude is vital. Remember that you have survived medical school, you got through the selection process to get onto your training scheme, and you have had specific training for the exam. You are reading this book so you know what to expect and how to prepare. You might have been on a course. Visualise the CSA as a challenge rather than as a threat — it is a highly valid exam, testing real life skills a GP needs. It is also highly reliable, meaning that if you are good enough you will pass.

## 5.15 On the day

### 5.15.1 Getting there

The CSA venue is 'No 1 Croydon', a purpose-adapted centre in Croydon in the southern suburbs of London. It is well served by public transport, but parking in the area is very limited. Make sure you plan your journey well in advance. If you are sitting the CSA in the morning you would be well advised to travel to London and stay overnight the night before. The south east of England is a busy place and transport systems are stretched, as a result any problem tends to result in lots of knock-on delays, so make sure you do not cut it too fine.

Make sure you have a mobile phone with you and the contact number the College have given you. If you are going to be delayed telephone and speak to the admin staff to let them know what has happened and when you think you are likely to arrive. They will do their best to accommodate you or reschedule your exam, but you will appreciate that this may not always be possible. Occasionally candidates or their close relatives get ill or there are significant life events — again telephone the College as soon as you suspect there might be a problem.

The other aspects to getting there relate to what sort of condition you are in when you get there! Make sure you are not getting there sleep-deprived or hung over. In the final few days before the exam there is little you can do in reality to improve your chances of passing. Very little of the CSA is knowledge-based so last minute revision really is not going to help much and can just add to the stress.

Plan a relaxing evening before the exam — if you are travelling to London make sure you arrive in plenty of time to unwind and get a good night's sleep. We all have different ways of relaxing whether it be via exercise, reading or socialising — choose what works for you. Perhaps think twice about going for that really spicy curry you like unless you are confident you have a cast iron constitution!

Most of us perform best if we are well nourished, so make sure you can arrange to have breakfast or lunch before going to the exam. However do not eat too much as it will make you sleepy.

What you wear is not desperately important; wear what you would normally wear for surgery. It is a professional exam but dressing over formally can affect the consultation, so there is no real need for a suit but on the converse turning up in jeans and a t-shirt probably is not going to inspire the patients with much confidence in you.

### 5.15.2 When you get there

When you get to the exam centre the College's administrative staff will greet you and register you. You will need some photographic proof of identity such as photo driving licence or passport. If you do forget it the college staff will do their best to accommodate you to allow you to produce it later, but it is the kind of stress you can do without.

You will also be asked to sign a non-disclosure agreement stating that you will not pass on information about the cases to anyone else. The College takes this very seriously and any breaches could be considered a professional issue with significant consequences.

You will be shown into a waiting room with the other candidates — in Croydon there will be three 'circuits' of the exam running at once, each of which will have at least twelve candidates, so there will be up to 40 or so of you. There is a cloakroom and lockers for you to store valuables and any items you are not permitted to take into the exam with you.

Be aware of what suits you best — perhaps you would rather sit quietly or perhaps that just makes you more stressed. You might take some light reading, or engage in conversation (about non-exam related things!) with a fellow-candidate.

There will be a briefing before you are shown to your consulting room. This will be delivered by one of the senior examiners and as well as clarifying what you should expect it will remind you of the exam regulations. These will be rigorously enforced and anyone found cheating risks disqualification. You will be given the opportunity to ask questions at the end of the briefing, following which a marshal will lead you to your room — the marshals are also senior examiners so will also be able to answer questions for you if need be.

Once in your room you will have a little time to settle down and get your equipment ready. You can also read the briefing instructions on your desk and have a look at the patient notes — they will be arranged in the order in which you will see the patients. Do you benefit from looking through the whole list? You have probably noticed for yourself that knowing who is coming to see you in a surgery can be off-putting if you notice a couple of heartsink patients in the list, and the same applies here. My advice is to read the notes for the first patient and leave it at that. There will not be much in the patient notes: you will be given their name, age and sex, any significant past history and any recent history of note or relevant investigation results or hospital letters and/or investigations.

### 5.15.3 Equipment

You are allowed to take a normal doctor's bag with its usual contents into the exam with you. This includes a stethoscope, otoscope, ophthalmoscope, etc. You are also allowed to take in a *BNF* or *MIMS*, and you will be sent a comprehensive list of what is allowed and what is not when you apply for the exam and you will be reminded in the briefing. Generally speaking you are not allowed any other books, protocols or guidelines, and you are not allowed any electronic equipment, including mobile phones.

You are allowed to take a desktop clock into your room with you to help you keep track of time, but do not attempt to set any alerts, for example to give you a warning 'bleep' at nine minutes, as it is distracting to the role-player as well as to yourself.

If you get there and find you have forgotten something, do not panic! If it comes to a physical examination role-play it and explain that you have forgotten your equipment. It is unlikely to influence your marks.

### 5.15.4 Behaving naturally

The key to performing on the day is to simply be a good doctor. Concentrate on the skills we have discussed in this chapter and try to be as relaxed and natural as you can. Concentrate entirely on the patient and ignore the assessor who will do their best to be unobtrusive and keep out of your line of sight. Do not look to the assessor for cues; imagine it is just you and the patient in the room.

You will naturally feel nervous, possibly very nervous, but remind yourself that it is entirely to be expected and that everyone else is in the same boat! Remember also that a degree of stress heightens alertness and can improve performance, so do not perceive your nervousness as a negative. It will usually settle within seconds of the first patient coming into your room in any case.

Be nice to the patient, decide how to introduce yourself and smile — it will make you feel better as well as the patient.

You will be really surprised how natural it can feel. The role-players are very good, the cases are realistic and well written and you will feel like you are in a real consultation. Do not try to second guess what the examiners want from you, just concentrate on doing your level best for the patient in front of you. There are no tricks or traps, and any hidden agendas will be realistic and if you give them a chance. The role-players will give you ample opportunity to spot them.

Do not try to think what the College 'party line' is on issues, just concentrate on good medical practice as appropriate for a normal GP.

### 5.15.5 The actual surgery

At the start of the surgery there will be a bell or buzzer and your first patient will knock and walk in. While you are greeting the patient the examiner will come in behind them and take a seat towards the back of the room. They should be positioned so that they are not in either your or the patient's immediate line of sight. They are briefed not to greet you or make eye contact, so do not feel offended and do not try to engage with them.

You can write on the paperwork provided, but be aware that it can be distracting for the patient as well as for yourself. You do not need to keep any record of the consultation and anything you write will not be seen by the assessor or contribute to your marks in any way. You have no computer to worry about and no risk of telephone interruptions so you have no excuses for giving the patient anything less than 100% of your attention.

You will have 13 consultations in total, of which 12 will be marked and the other will be a case that is being piloted. You will not know which one that is, so do not worry about it and consider them all equally important. It is possible that you will have a video camera in your room. The purpose of this is for quality control and training purposes, to allow the examiners to check that a case is working as planned, to monitor the role-players' performances and the calibration of the assessors. It is not there to record your performance.

After the ten minutes is up there will be another bell or buzzer to mark the end of the consultation. You need to close the consultation quickly — it is no good keeping on talking trying to get a few last points in because if you do that the role-player will simply get up and leave, and in any case the assessor is not likely to give you any credit for a few quick garbled instructions. It is best to simply say goodbye.

Remember to relax between patients and focus on the next patient you are going to see rather than dwell on the last one. Think about how you are going to approach the next patient, or even think about something completely unrelated such as what you are going to do when you get home. You will have a couple of minutes break before the next patient comes in as it takes a little time for the assessor to complete the mark sheet and move on to the next consulting room with the role-player. Occasionally it may take a little longer, and occasionally there are problems with paperwork or a role-player or the examiner might need to be swapped around. Do not worry, just stay in your room and wait. Familiarise yourself with the notes for the next patient.

At the halfway point there will be a refreshment break. Wait in your room until a marshal collects you to take you to the refreshment area for tea/coffee and biscuits. There are also toilet facilities in this area. The break will last between 20 and 30 minutes, during which time you may chat with your fellow candidates, however an invigilator will be present to make sure you do not discuss the cases. You will not be allowed to use your mobile phone during the break.

At the end of the surgery you should wait in your room until a marshal tells you may leave. Make sure you gather all your bits of equipment and collect your belongings from your locker. You must not remove any of the paperwork from your desk, and this includes any rough notes you have made — the College takes the security of the case bank very seriously.

### 5.15.6 Concerns

Rarely things happen that you feel might have compromised your ability to perform well in the exam. This could be something to do with the role-player's behaviour or performance, the assessor's behaviour or something entirely extraneous. While the role-players and assessors are highly professional, they are also human, so you do need to be realistic about this. If the role-player does make a slip or perform sub-optimally the assessor will almost certainly notice this before you do and will compensate for this in the grading. Similarly role-players and assessors get minor illnesses like colds and hayfever and you may need to accept a bit of sniffing or sneezing for example.

If you do feel something has affected your performance, however, it is best to ask to speak to the marshal — there will be a senior marshal on each circuit of the exam and they will listen to and note your concerns. It is best to do this either during the break in the middle of the surgery or at the end. They will do their best to rectify any problems at the time, but if that is not possible they will document it and take it up and correspond with you later. The MRCGP exam has always had an impeccable reputation for fairness and all those involved want it to remain that way.

## 5.16 After the exam

It could well be that the CSA is the last part of your exam. In any case it will still be an anti-climax after all the preparation. A long train journey home alone can be a bit miserable after a stressful experience, so investigate if you have the opportunity to meet up with friends or have your partner meet you for an evening out in London. If you have friends sitting the CSA at the same time as you then you will inevitably have a debrief, but again it is best not to dwell on your perceived mistakes and missed opportunities.

It is inevitable that you will discuss the cases you have encountered with your colleagues back in your practice and on your training scheme, but there is a difference between having a chat about the cases and actually trying to create a written record of them. In addition to the non-disclosure agreement you have signed, it is unprofessional to attempt to compromise the exam. The reason the College wants to maintain the confidentiality of the case bank is to maintain the fairness of the exam. Another point is that the cases in the CSA case bank number in the hundreds and are rotated regularly so your friends are unlikely to see the same cases anyway and could waste their time and effort on working up cases they will never see. As I pointed out previously, there is even a risk that knowing a case might compromise a candidate's performance.

Hopefully you will be able to celebrate when the results come out. It is a very rewarding feeling when you pass a challenging exam, and although the CSA 'is' challenging, hopefully you will regard it as having been a fair and valid assessment of your abilities as a GP. Of course passing the nMRCGP is actually a starting point not only for your career in general practice but also for your membership of the Royal College of General Practitioners. The RCGP is unique amongst the medical Royal Colleges in having a highly devolved organisation with local Faculties. Why not get involved with your local Faculty? Most Faculty Boards are only too delighted to see enthusiastic young GPs getting involved.

Good luck!

## References

Balint M (2000) *The Doctor, his Patinet and the Illness. 2nd edn*. Churchill Livingstone, London

Byrne PS, Long BEL (1976) *Doctors Talking to Patients*. Royal College of General Practitioners, London

Edwards A, Elwyn G, Mulley A (2002) Explaining risks: turning numerical data into meaningful pictures. *BMJ* 324: 827-30

Elyn G, Edwards A, Gwyn R et al (1999) Towards a feasible model for shared decision-making: focus group study with general practice registrars. *BMJ* 319: 753-56

Neighbour R, et al (2004) *The Inner Consultation: How to Develop an Effective and Intuitive Consulting Style*. Radcliffe Publishing, London

Pendleton D, Schofield T Tate P, Havelock P (1984) *The Consultation — An Approach to Teaching and Learning*. Oxford University Press, Oxford

Scott NC, Davis RH (1979) The exceptional potential in each primary care consultation. *J R Coll Gen Pract* 29(2010: 201-5

Tate P (2006) *The Doctor's Communication Handbook*. Radcliffe Publishing Ltd, London

**Resources**

**Breaking Bad News**: www.breakingbadnews.co.uk

**General Medical Council**: www.gmc-uk.org

**Royal College of General Practitioners**: www.rcgp.org.uk